Rodloi-- c

SECONDARY RESEARCH

Second Edition

Applied Social Research Methods Series
Volume 4

APPLIED SOCIAL RESEARCH METHODS SERIES

Series Editors:
LEONARD BICKMAN, Peabody College, Vanderbilt University, Nashville
DEBRA J. ROG, Vanderbilt University, Washington, DC

SECONDARY RESEARCH

Information Sources and Methods

Second Edition

David W. Stewart
Michael A. Kamins

Applied Social Research Methods Series
Volume 4

SAGE Publications
International Educational and Professional Publisher
Newbury Park   London   New Delhi

For information address:

SAGE Publications, Inc.
2455 Teller Road
Newbury Park, California 91320

SAGE Publications Ltd.
6 Bonhill Street
London EC2A 4PU
United Kingdom

SAGE Publications India Pvt. Ltd.
M-32 Market
Greater Kailash I
New Delhi 110 048 India

Printed in the United States of America

Library of Congress Cataloging-in-Publication Data

Stewart, David W.
  Secondary research : information sources and methods / David W.
Stewart, Michael A. Kamins. —2nd ed.
        p. cm. —(Applied social research methods series ; 4)
  Includes bibliographical references and index.
  ISBN 0-8039-5036-5 (cl.). —ISBN 0-8039-5037-3 (pb.)
  1. Social sciences—Research. I. Kamins, Michael A. II. Title.
III. Series: Applied social research methods series : v. 4.
H62.S7547   1993
300'.72—dc20   92-35501

93 94 95 96 10 9 8 7 6 5 4 3 2 1

Sage Production Editor: Tara S. Mead

Contents

Preface to Second Edition

When the first edition of this book appeared in 1984, the storage and acquisition of information were still essentially manual tasks. Computers were just making their presence felt. Thus much of the first edition of this book was devoted to the use of libraries and printed directories. Today libraries and printed source materials are still important, but they have been complemented by computer-assisted storage and retrieval systems. This has made the researcher's task easier, faster, more convenient, and less costly in time and money. At the same time, it has increased the amount of information that can be accessed. The latter event has added to the burden of evaluating and interpreting information. Thus the computer has changed the nature of the researcher's task, but it probably has not diminished the total effort required for a thorough analysis of secondary sources.

The second edition of the book is very similar to the first in its organization. It begins in Chapter 1 by defining secondary sources and by providing a quick introduction to the task of secondary analysis. This is followed by a discussion and evaluation of secondary sources in Chapter 2. This discussion is followed by several chapters that provide an introduction to specific information sources, including government and commercial sources. Two chapters are devoted to computer-based information—on-line information search services and the more recent CD-ROM products. The book concludes with a chapter that provides examples of information searches and a chapter on the analysis, integration, and interpretation of secondary sources.

Information sources have increased greatly in number since the first edition. This added to the task of attempting to update the book while keeping its length close to the original. Also adding to the task of updating the book are the very rapid changes that are occurring in the information industry. New products are being introduced daily, as others disappear. The publishing and research industries have experienced significant change and consolidation in recent years, and this consolidation continues. These changes make it inevitable that portions of this book will become quickly out-of-date, but an effort has been made to make as much of it as possible independent of time.

One important difference between the first and second editions is the addition of a second author. This provides an opportunity for a fresh look at the content and organization of the book. It also makes the task of updating source material easier.

We would be remiss if we did not offer our thanks to Len Bickman and Debra Rog, the editors of the Applied Social Research Methods Series at Sage. They goaded us into undertaking the revision effort. We also wish to thank the many individuals who have used the first edition of the book in their own research or in their classes. The comments of these individuals have been useful and relevant.

—David W. Stewart
Michael A. Kamins

1

Introduction

Secondary information consists of sources of data and other information collected by others and archived in some form. These sources include government reports, industry studies, archived data sets, and syndicated information services as well as the traditional books and journals found in libraries. Secondary information offers relatively quick and inexpensive answers to many questions and is almost always the point of departure for primary research.

Recently, a large multinational frozen foods company was considering entry into the in-home fried potato market in Japan. Of critical concern regarding the entry decision was a determination of the per capita household consumption of frozen potatoes in the country, as well as some idea of the most recent consumption trend. It was evident that competitors also were considering entry, and hence a decision had to be made rather quickly.

One could approach this issue by conducting a nationwide survey of Japanese households. Such a perspective, however, would be extremely costly and time-consuming. A more efficient, more timely, and less costly approach might be to consult relevant existing sources of international statistical information relating to this issue. Hence the researcher could begin the search with a publication such as *Index to International Statistics: A Guide to the Statistical Publications of International Intergovernmental Organizations,* published by the Congressional Information Service. The point to be made here is that not every study or research undertaking must begin with the collection of primary data (i.e., data originated by the researcher for the purpose of the investigation at hand). In this case, the information required was already available from published sources. Given the potential entry of competitors into the market, the need to obtain information quickly, the cost of conducting a survey, and the fact that the information already existed, the use of published sources was a wise choice.

The wisdom of using existing data in the example above may seem obvious. Use of existing data requires knowledge of their existence and the means for accessing them, however, as well as the time and effort to acquire them. Such information is not always identified easily. Most social scientists have little familiarity with the vast array of information available to them. At the same time, the use of published information is a mainstay of virtually every research effort. Such information sources are called *secondary data*. These data were collected for some general information need or as a part of a research effort designed to answer a specific question. Secondary data come in many forms, ranging from large statistical studies published by the government and other organizations to the unpublished observations of a knowledgeable observer.

A vast international information industry has come into being since the 1950s. This industry obtains, stores, and even sells information in one form or another. Today, with the advent of compact disk read-only memory (CD-ROM) technology, one disk places information that would fill as much as 1,800 floppy disks literally in the palm of your hand. To say the least, these recent changes in information technology have added great power to the capacity of individuals and organizations to identify and use information. Indeed, such changes may have affected the way we do research. With secondary data now so easily accessible, their use should only continue to expand.

The raw data collected by others may often be available to the general public, but more likely these data are summarized and reported in concise form. Such published summaries are often referred to as *secondary sources*. The term *secondary information* is used frequently to refer to both secondary data (the raw data obtained in various studies) and secondary sources (the published summaries of these data). In the remainder of this book, these terms will be used interchangeably, because the distinction among these types of information tends to blur in practice. The use of secondary information often is referred to as *secondary analysis* (or research). Secondary analysis is simply a further analysis of information that already has been obtained. Such an analysis may be related to the original purpose for which the data were collected, or it may address an issue quite different from that which prompted the original data-gathering effort. It may involve the integration of information from several sources or a reanalysis of the data from a single source.

Most research efforts begin with some type of secondary analysis. An investigation of secondary sources provides an opportunity to learn what is already known, and what remains to be learned, about a particular topic. It may suggest methods for studying a particular problem. It is often possible to combine the information from several different sources to reach conclusions that are not suggested by any one source.

Indeed, theory building in the social sciences frequently takes the form of integrating the findings of multiple empirical studies within a single general framework.

Secondary research differs from *primary research* in that the collection of the information is not the responsibility of the analyst. In secondary research, the analyst enters the picture after the data collection effort is over. In primary research, the analyst is responsible for the design of the research, the collection of the data, and the analysis and summary of the information. In some situations, primary and secondary research are substitutes for each other. For example, if one were interested in the transportation habits of individuals in a large metropolitan area, a survey of a representative sample of the residents of the area could be taken. Such a survey would involve primary research. The analyst might design a questionnaire requesting information about the use of various modes of transportation, types of trips taken during some time interval, preference for various means of transportation, and other relevant information. The survey instrument (questionnaire) would be mailed to a sample of residents of the metropolitan area. As the questionnaires were returned, the analyst would tabulate responses and summarize the data.

An alternative method for investigating the same issue might involve secondary research. If a study of the transportation habits of the metropolitan area had been conducted recently by someone else, it might be possible to answer all of the questions about transportation habits by referring to that study. In fact, the U.S. Bureau of the Census carries out a census of transportation that includes a survey of transportation habits. Rather than conducting his or her own study, the analyst may use the data collected by the Census Bureau. Use of Census Bureau data has the advantages of being less expensive and providing answers more quickly than primary research. The disadvantage of using this secondary source is that questions of interest may not be addressed in the Census Bureau survey or may have been asked in a fashion that is not consistent with the analyst's current interests.

More often, primary and secondary research are used in a complementary fashion, rather than as substitutes for one another. Research efforts generally begin with a question or set of objectives. These objectives are met and the question answered through the acquisition of information. The source of the information—whether it is obtained by secondary or primary research—is really not important as long as the information is trustworthy and answers the question at hand. In fact, it will be less expensive and time-consuming to use secondary sources. Frequently, however, at least some of the questions at hand have not been answered by prior research; answering these questions requires primary research. In these cases, secondary research helps define the agenda for subsequent primary research by suggesting which questions require answers that have not been obtained in previous research. Secondary data may also identify the means by which the primary research should be carried out in terms of questions that should be addressed, measurement instruments (e.g., questionnaires), and relevant respondents.

In applied settings, such as government agencies, corporations, and other organizations, information is required for administrative decisions. Because there is generally some cost associated with obtaining information by primary research, it is more efficient to use secondary research when it is available. Identifying what is already known and available in secondary sources also ensures that funds are expended only for the acquisition of new information. A thorough knowledge of secondary information tends to enhance the efficiency of primary research efforts.

Curiously, many individuals and organizations do not take full advantage of the secondary information available to them. This is in part the result of the information explosion that has occurred in the last 20 years and the lack of systematic guides to secondary sources. As noted earlier, however, the recent introduction of CD-ROM technology may change all of this. Indeed, it is difficult to conceive of a research effort that does not begin with at least some secondary research. Existing information provides a foundation for problem formulation, for the design of new research, and for the analysis and interpretation of new information. There is little point in rediscovering that which is known already. The purpose of primary research generally should be to fill gaps in existing knowledge. These gaps cannot be identified without an understanding of the existing knowledge base.

It is perhaps unfortunate that the term *secondary* has been chosen to refer to existing data. This term does not imply anything about the importance of the information, only that it is being used for research beyond the specific informational need that prompted the original gathering of the data. All primary research may ultimately become someone else's secondary source. In the remainder of this book, secondary sources will be examined. Specific sources and how they might be used will be addressed, but first the advantages of secondary information will be discussed.

ADVANTAGES OF SECONDARY INFORMATION

Secondary information has some distinctive advantages over primary data collection efforts. The most significant of these advantages are related to time and cost. In general, it is much less expensive to use secondary data than it is to conduct a primary research investigation. This is true even when there are costs associated with obtaining the secondary data. When answers to questions are required quickly, the only practical alternative is to consult secondary sources. If stringent budget and time constraints are imposed on primary research, secondary research may provide higher-quality data than could be obtained with a new research project.

Secondary sources provide a useful starting point for additional research by suggesting problem formulations, research hypotheses, and research methods. Consultation of secondary sources provides a means for increasing the efficiency of the research dollar by targeting real gaps and oversights in knowledge. Secondary data also may provide a useful comparative tool. New data may be compared to existing data for purposes of examining differences or trends. They also may provide a basis for determining whether or not the new information is representative of a population, as in the case of sampling. Comparison of the demographic characteristics of a sample to those of the larger population, as specified by the Bureau of the Census, may reveal how representative the sample is of the larger population.

DISADVANTAGES OF SECONDARY INFORMATION

On September 12, 1989, a headline in the *Boston Globe* read, "SAT Scores of Most Ethnic Groups Improved in '89, College Board Says." On that same day, the *New York Times* reported that "Minority Students Gain on College Entrance Tests," while the Tarrytown, NY, *Daily News* claimed that "SAT Scores Take Dip for Women, Minorities." A report in the *Wall Street Journal* covered the more general results of the test, claiming that "Scores on College Entrance Tests Fall." *USA TODAY* essentially disagreed with this statement, reporting that "SAT Scores End '80s Up." Finally, the *Chicago Tribune* reported on that fateful day that "College Entrance Scores Slip to a 5-Year Low."[1]

Given all of the above information, one can only ask: What's the score? This example clearly illustrates the potential problems inherent in the collection, reporting, and interpretation of secondary information. Data often are collected with a specific purpose in mind, a purpose that may produce deliberate or unintentional bias. As Reichmann (1962) notes:

> Newspapers do not assist in the interpretation of results, for they invariably select what appear to be the most significant points and emphasize these at the expense of tabulations and supporting notes. The latter are rarely, if ever, published. This in itself is not a criticism of the press since it is their function to draw attention to occurrences and not necessarily to describe them in full. (p. 261)

In addition, the data collected might be so extensive that the individual whose job it is to interpret the findings can potentially arrive at many different, even conflicting conclusions, all of which might be supported by some subset of the data. As Reichmann (1962) again notes, "Some reports do, however, actually misinterpret and emphasize quite erroneous conclusions, thus helping to bring statistics into unjustified disrepute." Thus secondary sources must be evaluated carefully. Chapter 2 is devoted to the evaluation of secondary information.

The fact that secondary data were collected originally for particular purposes may produce other problems. Category definitions, particular measures, or treatment effects may not be the most appropriate for the purpose at hand. Seldom are secondary data available at the individual-observation level. This means that the data are aggregated in some form, and the unit of aggregation may be inappropriate for a particular purpose. Finally, secondary data are, by definition, old data. Thus the data may not be particularly timely for some purposes. This is a major problem for census data, which may not be published in its entirety for at least 2 years after the collection process is completed.

SOURCES OF SECONDARY DATA

Secondary data are available from a variety of sources and in a variety of forms, although the largest and most frequently consulted source is a library. Libraries differ in the kinds of materials they have available. University libraries tend to carry academically relevant materials. Public libraries carry more general interest and business-relevant materials. Government libraries handle government documents, and commercial libraries carry documents of interest to clients. Many commercial organizations, corporations, and research firms also maintain their own specialized libraries, which they may allow others to use. The single best guide to a library is its reference librarian. This individual is a specialist with training in information sources who can provide guidance to the most relevant information for a particular purpose. Many organizations have information officers or librarians whose function it is to assist others in locating information. Public and commercial libraries have developed information hot lines for their patrons' specific questions. Many libraries are responsive to their users' needs for various information resources and welcome suggestions.

University and public libraries do not carry academic literature only. There is a substantial amount of information produced by government agencies, corporations, trade and professional organizations, and other organizations that many libraries will carry. These sources can be quite general, as in the case of government census data, or quite specific, as in the case of trade journals such as *Beverage World* or *Progressive Grocer.* The magnitude of available information necessitates access to general guides and indices to this literature. These guides represent an important access point to secondary literature. Table 1.1 provides a listing of some of the more common guides and directories to general secondary sources. Guides to the more specialized academic literature sources are described in Table 1.2. The sources listed in these two tables represent good starting points for a library search, but libraries are not the only sources of secondary information. There are many others, including the following:

1. Experts and authorities. A good starting point for learning about a topic is someone who is well acquainted with the topic, perhaps someone who has been involved in research on the topic. For example, one researcher, after an exhaustive search of the biological and veterinary medicine literature, finally obtained the information he needed by telephoning veterinary schools until he located an authority on the topic. The information required was simple (how much food an adult cat consumes in a day), but was essential for estimating the market potential for a new pet food.

Trade and professional associations, chambers of commerce, executives, and researchers are all important sources of information. Much valuable information consists of information obtained through experience. Sorted impressions and conclusions based on experience are often the only sources of information on some topics. A few telephone calls

Text continued on page 12

Table 1.1

General Directories and Guides to Secondary Source Material

American Statistics Index (ASI)

A comprehensive guide to the statistical publications of the U.S. government. It also features an index by categories that includes references to all publications that contain comparative tabular data broken down into designated geographic, economic, and demographic categories. The ASI has been published annually (with monthly and quarterly updates) since 1973 by the Congressional Information Service, Washington, DC.

Applied Sciences and Technology Index

A subject index to more than 325 journals in aeronautics, automation, chemistry, computer technology, energy, engineering, fire and fire prevention, food and food industries, geology, machinery, mathematics, metallurgy, oceanography, petroleum and gas, physics, plastics, space science, textiles and fabrics, transportation, and so forth. The index, edited by Joyce Howard, is published monthly and in a quarterly and annual cumulation by H. W. Wilson Co., New York.

Bibliographic Guide to Business and Economics

A comprehensive listing by author, title, and subject of books, reports, and conference papers regarding business, economics, finance, labor, and related fields. Catalogued since 1975 by the Library of Congress and the New York Public Library, Research Library, New York.

Business Index

An index providing subject coverage of 830 business periodicals and newspapers as well as business information from approximately 1,500 general and legal periodicals, edited by Delores Meglio and published monthly since 1979 by Information Access Company, Foster City, CA.

Business Information: A Guide for Librarians, Students and Researchers

This book is divided into two parts. The first part covers business information according to the format in which it is made available: guides, bibliographies, quick reference sources, directories, periodicals and newspapers, loose-leaf services, government documents, statistics, vertical file materials, and data bases. The second part of the text focuses on specific business disciplines, addressing marketing, accounting and taxation, money, credit and banking investment (with separate chapters for stocks, bonds, mutual funds, and futures/options), insurance, and real estate. Written by Diane W. Strauss, it was published in 1988 by Libraries Unlimited, Inc., Englewood, CO.

Business Information: How to Find It, How to Use It

This guide emphasizes research techniques and basic business concepts as well as information sources. Four special topics are covered in depth: marketing, business law, tax law, and gathering business information for job hunters and consumers. Written by Michael Lavin, it was published in 1987 by Oryx Press, Phoenix, AZ.

Business Information Sources

Lists and annotates a vast array of books, periodicals, documents, data bases, and other sources. It is divided into two main parts. The first part describes basic business reference sources. The second focuses on specific management functions, covering disciplines such as accounting, corporate finance and banking, international management, insurance, real estate, and marketing. The revised edition was published in 1985 by the University of California Press, Berkeley, CA.

Table 1.1 Continued

Business Periodicals Index
The principal content of this publication is an annotated index of articles from 345 business periodicals, including book reviews, and a biographical index. It is available on CD-ROM for a $1,495 annual subscription and on-line through Wilsonline. The index, edited by Walter Webb, has been published monthly (with an annual cumulation) since 1959 by H. W. Wilson Co., New York.

Business Reference Sources
An annotated guide for Harvard Business School students, compiled by Lorna M. Daniells. It provides a selective bibliography of indexes and abstracts, directories, financial sources, basic U.S. statistical sources, statistics for industry analysis, guides to statistics and industry data, market research sources, and international statistics. Available through the Baker Library, Graduate School of Business, Harvard.

Directories in Print
Formally known as the *Directory of Directories,* the eighth annual edition appeared in 1991 in two volumes. Indexed by subject matter and title, it is an annotated guide to more than 14,000 directories published worldwide, including business and industrial directories; professional and scientific rosters; entertainment, recreation, and cultural directories; directory data bases; and other nonprofit products. Edited by Charles B. Montney and published by Gale Research, Inc., Detroit, MI.

Encyclopedia of Associations
This publication provides detailed entries describing more than 22,000 active associations, organizations, clubs, and other nonprofit membership groups across many disciplines and fields. Descriptive information and basic contact data are provided for each association listed. In 1991, the 25th edition was published. Edited by Deborah M. Durek and published by Oryx Press, Phoenix, AZ.

Encyclopedia of Business Information Sources
The seventh edition of this publication appeared in 1988. Information sources are presented under 1,000 key business subjects; for each subject, a detailed listing of live, print, and electronic sources is provided. The 1989 update adds entries for 50 new subjects and 20 subjects listed previously. Topics covered include advertising, business forecasting, investments, management theory, marketing, and telemarketing. Edited by James Woy and published by Gale Research, Inc., Detroit, MI.

Encyclopedia of Geographic Information Sources
This two-volume set (U.S. volume published in 1986; international volume published in 1988) supplies contact information for both live and printed information sources. City information sources include newspapers, chambers of commerce, and guidebooks. Country listings include information agencies and organizations, as well as bibliographic data on 12 types of publications. Edited by Jennifer Mossman and published by Gale Research, Inc., Detroit, MI.

Marketing Information: A Professional Reference Guide
This guide provides a directory to associations and organizations arranged by broad subject classifications. It also briefly annotates books, manuals, directories, periodicals, newsletters, data bases, and nonprint materials arranged by subject areas such as pricing, physical distribution, and sales promotion. Written by Jack L. Goldstucker and Otto Echemendia, it was published in 1987 by the Georgia State University College of Business Administration.

(Continued)

Table 1.1 Continued

Monthly Catalog of U.S. Government Publications
A listing of the publications of the U.S. government, published since 1895.

Public Affairs Information Service Bulletin
A biweekly subject index to books, pamphlets, government documents, periodical articles, and other publications related to socioeconomic conditions and public affairs.

Readers' Guide to Periodical Literature
A directory containing subject and author indexes of approximately 200 general publications in the United States, published semimonthly since 1900.

Standard Periodical Directory
Published in its 14th edition in 1991, it provides data and descriptions of more than 75,000 periodicals in the United States and Canada. Edited by Matthew Manning and published by Oxbridge Communications, Inc., New York.

Statistical Reference Index (SRI)
A guide to American statistical publications from private organizations and state government sources. Published monthly (with annual contributions) since 1980 by the Congressional Information Service, Washington, DC.

Statistics Sources
This is a subject guide for data on industrial, business, social, educational, financial, and other topics for the United States and foreign countries. Edited by Jacqueline Wasserman O'Brien and Steven R. O'Brien and published in 1989 by Gale Research, Inc., Detroit, MI.

Ulrich's International Business Directory
Covers more than 116,000 serials currently published throughout the world under 668 subject headings. Appearing on an annual basis since 1932, it is published by R. R. Bowker, New York; Edvika Pupilskis is the senior editor.

Table 1.2
Guides to Academic Literature

America: History and Life
An index published in three parts: (a) article abstracts and citations, (b) index to book reviews, and (c) American history bibliography. This book indexes articles on ethnic studies, folklore, history, politics and government, urban affairs. and related topics. It is available on-line and is published by the American Bibliographical Center and Clio Press, Santa Barbara, CA.

Business Ethics and Responsibility: An Information Sourcebook
This is a guide to the literature on business ethics, focusing primarily on books and journal articles. Emphasis is on business literature; more than 1,000 references are cited. Written by Patricia Ann Bick and edited by Paul Wasserman, it is published by Oryx Press, Phoenix, AZ (Series on Business and Management).

Communication Abstracts
A quarterly index of major articles, books, and monographs related to communication. Abstracts on indexed publications are included.

Table 1.2 Continued

Current Index to Journals in Education (CIJE)
An index to articles in approximately 800 journals in education and related fields. Published monthly with semiannual and annual cumulations by Oryx Press, Phoenix, AZ (available on fiche).

Dissertation Abstracts International
A publication in two volumes: (a) the humanities and social sciences, and (b) sciences and engineering. It includes titles, key words, and author indices for doctoral dissertations from more than 350 institutions in the United States and abroad. Abstracts of the dissertations are provided. It has been published monthly, in several sections, since 1952. Complete copies of dissertations may be ordered from University Microfilms, Ann Arbor, MI.

Education Index
This is a monthly subject and author index to 350 education publications, yearbooks, and monographs, with quarterly and annual cumulations. Edited by Mary Louise Hewitt and published by H. W. Wilson Co., New York (available on-line).

Engineering Index Monthly
A monthly guide to engineering literature (available on-line).

Historical Abstracts
Comprising two volumes (twentieth-century abstracts and modern history abstracts), this publication abstracts and indexes periodicals in history, including international periodicals (available on-line).

Human Resources Abstracts (formerly *Poverty and Human Resources*)
An abstract journal of Sage Publications providing coverage of human resource and social problems and solutions, ranging from slum rehabilitation and job development training to compensatory education, minority group problems, and rural poverty.

Index Medicus
This is a bibliographic listing of references to current articles from some 2,600 of the world's biomedical journals. It includes subject/author sections.

Index to Health Information
This is a guide to government, intergovernmental, and private health publications. Published by the Congressional Information Service, Bethesda, MD.

Index to Legal Periodicals
A guide to the literature on law and the judicial system. Lists articles in 475 publications by subject and author. Published quarterly with annual cumulations by George Washington University, Washington, DC (available on-line).

Management Contents
Contains abstracts on a wide range of business- and management-related publications, including conference proceedings. Covers approximately 350 business and management journals.

Market Research Abstracts
Provides abstracts of marketing articles appearing in marketing journals around the world. Published on a semiannual basis since 1963 by the London Market Research Society.

Mental Health Abstracts
Abstracts of publications related to mental health. Sources include more than 15,000 journals in 41 countries.

(Continued)

Table 1.2 Continued

Personnel Management Abstracts
Provides one-paragraph abstracts of selected articles and books and a comprehensive index of authors, titles, and subjects.

Population Bibliography
Indexes journals, technical reports, government reports, and other publications related to demography.

Psychological Abstracts
Provides abstracts of articles from more than 1,200 periodicals and 2,000 books in psychology and related areas. Now available on-line as "PsychInfo."

Sage Public Administration Abstracts
An index of publications related to public administration. Abstracts of papers are included.

Science Citation Index
Comparable to the SSCI (see below), but for the natural sciences. Includes approximately 90% of the significant scientific and technical literature published worldwide.

Social Science Citation Index (SSCI)
Indexes the significant items from approximately 1,200 worldwide social and behavioral science journals and selected articles from about 2,800 journals in the natural, physical, and biomedical sciences. Includes a citation index, author index (first author only), and subject index. Published by the Institute for Scientific Information since 1969.

Social Science Index
A subject and author index to articles in more than 300 journals in the social and behavioral sciences, law, medicine, and related subjects.

Sociological Abstracts
Provides abstracts of articles related to sociology in 33 main topic areas. More than 1,500 journals in sociology and related disciplines are covered. Published by Sociological Abstracts, Inc., San Diego, CA.

United States Political Science Documents
Provides abstracts and indexing for approximately 175 major U.S. journals related to political science.

Work Related Abstracts
Annotated index of books, articles, and dissertations covering labor relations, personnel management, and organizational behavior.

to knowledgeable experts are sometimes all that is required to obtain a piece of information, and there are situations in which such expert opinion is the *only* source of information. Clearly, however, such information must be evaluated carefully, and opinion separated from fact. This is not always accomplished easily, particularly in the case of value-laden topics. A good question to ask such experts is how they know something to be the case.

2. Recorded data and records. Nearly every organization generates data as a normal part of its operations. Letters, memoranda, sales contracts, purchase orders, service orders, client or patient records, accounting records, and so on are all potentially valuable sources of information. Such information is not always accessible, but often it is. Usually, however, such information must be reorganized and reanalyzed in a different form. This is particularly true of routine operating information from organizations.

3. Commercial information services. Numerous firms are in the business of collecting and selling information. Such information may be available in published summary form, but it also may be available as raw data. These summaries or raw data may be accessible in hard-copy format, or they may be accessible through electronic networks. Such information is unlikely to be available in libraries as long as it has commercial value. A variety of the information services offered by these firms will be reviewed in subsequent chapters. Although such information is costly, it is often less expensive and more practical to use than information obtained by doing a comparable study of one's own.

4. CD-ROM. The need to access information quickly and reliably has grown hand in hand with the adoption of home and laptop computers. Compact disk read-only memory (CD-ROM) technology gives the microcomputer user about 680 megabytes (the equivalent of almost 300 pages) of information on a single disk that resembles a music CD. Information is accessed quickly, and the user typically pays an annual subscription or a one-time fee for unlimited access. This technology will be covered in depth in a later chapter, but suffice it to say that many different data bases are now available on CD-ROM, including those that are classified as indexes, source, and reference in nature.

Many researchers approach the secondary research activity with trepidation. Until one has become familiar with them, libraries can be imposing operations, and there may be a sense of embarrassment associated with approaching experts in a given field. Once one is acquainted with how to access information, however, libraries become vital resources. Likewise, electronic retrieval of reports or data may require learning specialized commands in addition to knowing how to use computers and communications programs.

Secondary sources are a vital resource for all social scientists, but they may be more important for the applied researcher than for one engaged in more basic research. Basic research is concerned primarily with producing new knowledge and with filling gaps that exist in current knowledge. Secondary data thus serve as points of departure that the basic researcher seeks to go beyond. The applied researcher, on the other hand, more often is concerned with using knowledge that already exists, at least in some form, for the solution of a specific problem. For the applied researcher, primary research is required only when secondary information does not provide answers to specific questions. Thus, for the social scientist working in an applied setting, a familiarity with secondary sources is a prerequisite for successful practice (see Hedrick, Bickman, & Rog, 1992, for a more complete discussion of this point).

The remainder of this book is concerned with getting and using secondary information. Table 1.3 provides a brief guide to getting started when seeking secondary sources.

SUMMARY

Information is a vital resource for planning and decision making. Research scientists, business planners, and government policymakers all need skills for obtaining and using information that already exists. A tremendous store of information is available, and guides, directories, and other resources are also available for identifying this information. Computers have made information increasingly accessible, especially with the newly available CD-ROM technology. There is little excuse for not using secondary data. They provide an efficient and timely place to begin any research. For many purposes, secondary data may be the only type required.

EXERCISES

Exercise 1.1: Select a topic. Following the guidelines in Table 1.3, compile a list of references, directories, authorities, and other sources of information that you would consult for further information.

Exercise 1.2: Contact several business executives, administrators, or government officials. Learn what secondary sources they routinely consult in planning and decision making. Based on what you have learned, can you identify any sources of information that you think they should be consulting?

Table 1.3
Published Sources: How to Get Started

Step 1: Identify what you wish to know and what you already know about your topic. This may include relevant facts, names of researchers or organizations associated with the topic, key papers and other publications with which you are already familiar, and any other information you may have.

Step 2: Develop a list of key terms and names. These terms and names will provide access to secondary sources. Unless you already have a very specific topic of interest, keep this initial list long and quite general.

Step 3: Now you are ready to use the library. Begin your search with several of the directories and guides listed in Tables 1.1 and 1.2. If you know of a particularly relevant paper or author, start with the *Social Science Citation Index* (or *Science Citation Index*) and try to identify papers by the same author, or papers citing the author or work. At this stage it is probably not worthwhile to attempt an exhaustive search. Only look at the previous 2 or 3 years of work in the area, using three or four general guides. Some directories and indices use a specialized list of key terms or descriptors. Such indices often have thesauri that identify these terms. A search of these directories requires that your list of terms and descriptors be consistent with the thesauri.

Step 4: Compile the literature you have found. Is it relevant to your needs? Perhaps you are overwhelmed by information, or perhaps you have found little that is relevant. Rework your list of key words and authors.

Step 5: Continue your search in the library. Expand your search to include a few more years and one or two more sources. Evaluate your findings.

Step 6: At this point you should have a clear idea of the nature of the information you are seeking and sufficient background to use more specialized resources.

Step 7: Consult the reference librarian. You may wish to consider a computer-assisted information search, either on-line or through the use of CD-ROM materials. The reference librarian can assist you with such a search but will need your help, particularly for on-line applications, in the form of a carefully constructed list of key words. Some librarians will prefer to produce their own lists of key words or descriptors, but it is a good idea to verify that such a list is reasonably complete. The librarian may be able to suggest specialized sources related to the topic. Remember, the reference librarian cannot be of much help until you can provide some rather specific information about what you want to know.

Step 8: If you have had little success or your topic is highly specialized, consult *Business Information: A Guide for Librarians, Students and Researchers; Business Reference Sources; Directories in Print; Statistics Sources; Statistical Reference Index; American Statistics Index; Encyclopedia of Geographic Information Sources;* or one of the other guides to information listed in this book. These are really directories of directories, which means that this level of search will be very general. You will first need to identify potentially useful primary directories, which will then lead you to other sources.

Step 9: If you are unhappy with what you have found or are otherwise having trouble, and if the reference librarian has not been able to identify sources, use an authority. Identify some individual or organization that might know something about the

(Continued)

Table 1.3 Continued

topic. The various *Who's Who* publications, *Consultants and Consulting Organizations Directory, Encyclopedia of Associations, Industrial Research Laboratories in the United States,* or *Research Centers Directory* may help you to identify sources.

Step 10: Once you have identified sources that you wish to consult, you can determine whether they are readily available in your library. Interlibrary loan is a procedure whereby one library obtains materials from another. This is accomplished through a network of libraries that have agreed to provide access to their collections in return for the opportunity to obtain materials from other libraries in the network. Most libraries have an interlibrary loan form on which relevant information about requested materials is written. Interlibrary loans are generally made for some specific period (usually 1 or 2 weeks). Very specialized or rare publications may take some time to locate, but most materials requested are obtained within a couple of weeks. If you would like to purchase a particular work, consult *Ulrich's International Periodicals Directory, Irregular Serials and Annuals: An International Directory,* or *Books in Print* to determine whether a work is in print and where it may be obtained. Local bookstores often have computerized or microfilm inventories of book wholesalers and can provide rapid access to books and monographic items.

Step 11: Even after an exhaustive search of a library's resources, it is always possible that little information will be found. In such cases, it may be necessary to identify experts or other authorities who might provide the information you are seeking or suggest sources you have not identified or consulted. Identifying authorities is often a trial-and-error process. One might begin by calling a university department, government agency, or other organization that employs persons in the field of interest. Reference librarians often can suggest individuals who might be helpful. A large number of such calls, however, may be necessary before an appropriate expert is identified.

NOTE

2

Evaluating Secondary Sources

Not all information obtained from secondary sources is equally reliable or valid. In-formation must be evaluated carefully and weighted according to its recency and credibility. When evaluating secondary information, six questions must be answered: (1) What was the purpose of the study? (2) Who collected the information? (3) What information was actually collected? (4) When was the information collected? (5) How was the information obtained? (6) How consistent is the information with other sources?

The regular user of secondary information often develops a healthy skepticism about information provided by others. There are many ways that data may be misleading if they are not evaluated carefully. Data collection is usually purposive, and the purpose for which information is obtained and analyzed may influence the conclusions drawn, the data collection procedure employed, the definitions of terms and categories, and even the quality of the information. In addition, not all secondary sources, even those that appear on the surface to be relevant, are necessar-ily appropriate for a given purpose or analysis. A particular source may have information that is similar to what is needed, but may provide measures that use a different unit of analysis from that of interest, focus on a slightly different issue, or otherwise fail to provide the type of in-formation sought.

As an example, consider the case of *Tambrands vs. the Warner-Lambert Company*, makers of the home pregnancy test EPT Plus. Based upon a research study, Warner-Lambert made the advertised claim that their test gave results in "as soon as 10 minutes." Tambrands, a competitor, found this claim to be exaggerated and brought suit appropriately ques-tioning the validity of the research underlying the claim. In their de-fense, Warner-Lambert reported the results of a research study of 19 pregnant women who were selected to take the test. The findings revealed that 10, or 52.6%, obtained positive (i.e., pregnant) test results within the claimed 10 minutes; however, 2 women received these results within 30 minutes, and the remaining 7 recorded false negatives. The argument presented by Warner-Lambert was that their advertised claim was supported by the research findings because "the *overwhelming majority* of women . . . will in fact obtain accurate results in ten minutes, even on Day 1" (emphasis added). Tambrands countered by appropriately examining how the information was obtained and if reasonable conclusions were drawn from it.

The answer to the first question revealed that the 19 women sampled were actually enrolled at a Cincinnati fertility clinic, so the sample was not representative. Moreover, the claimed "overwhelming majority" of 52.6% was not revealed to be statistically significant from one half ($t = .23$, $p < .95$). Indeed, for such a result to be statistically significant from 50%, a sample of approximately 1,400 pregnant women would have had to be taken. Although the court recognized the questionable statistical validity of Warner-Lambert's data, it ruled against the company on the grounds that "the results . . . do not support the defendant's claims." If the survey results had been more supportive of Warner-Lambert, it is not clear that issues related to the validity of the study would have come to the forefront. *Thus the lesson to be learned is always to question the information collected and reported by others, as Tambrands did.* No data should be used without careful evaluation, and data obtained from secondary sources require especially close scrutiny.

The evaluation of secondary data should follow the same procedures employed in the evaluation of primary data. The researcher who uses secondary sources, however, does have an advantage. Because the information already exists in some form, evaluation of the quality and appropriateness of the information can be done well in advance of its actual use. Secondary data can be identified and evaluated in a stepwise fashion. Too often researchers wait until there is an immediate need for information before evaluating the appropriateness of existing sources. This leaves little time for careful evaluation and frequently affords no opportunity for searching for more appropriate sources. It is important for researchers who use secondary sources to identify them early and to clarify as much information as possible before beginning analysis.

Questions concerning the source(s) of the data (as above), the measures used, the time of data collection, and the appropriateness of analyses and conclusions should be raised routinely. The questions a user of secondary sources might raise can be grouped into six broad categories:

1. What was the purpose of the study? Why was the information collected?
2. Who was responsible for collecting the information? What qualifications, resources, and potential biases are represented in the conduct of the study?

3. What information was actually collected? How were units and concepts defined? How direct were the measures used? How complete was the information? Are there any differences in the quality of different variables?
4. When was the information collected? Is the information still current, or have events made the information obsolete? Were there specific events occurring at the time the data were collected that may have produced the particular results obtained?
5. How was the information obtained? What was the methodology employed in obtaining the data?
6. How consistent is the information obtained from one source with information available from other sources?

It is impossible to evaluate information without knowing the answers to each of these questions. One should be immediately suspicious of any information for which answers to these questions are unavailable. The importance of each of these questions is discussed in further detail in the remainder of this chapter.

WHAT WAS THE PURPOSE OF THE STUDY?

Information rarely is collected without some intent. The intent of a particular study may significantly influence the findings. Data collected to further the interests of a particular group or organization are especially suspect, as the example above suggested. The degree of precision, the types of categories used, and the method by which data are collected and reported are often dictated by the intent of the study.

Consider the following: To support their brand in a comparison against Winston Lights, Loews Theaters (makers of Triumph cigarettes) conducted a four-question consumer survey designed to examine the quality of its brand versus that of Winston. On two questions that measured "preference" and "better taste," Triumph fared better than its competition. On scales relating to "amount of taste" and "satisfying quality," however, this was not the case. In spite of this, Loews chose to base their advertising claim on the favorable results to the first two questions only, largely ignoring the remaining questions. This resulted in a lawsuit filed by R. J. Reynolds (manufacturer of Winston Lights) against Loews Theaters. The court ruled in favor of R. J. Reynolds because Triumph had "failed to establish a basis" on which to claim that only the first two questions had relevance to the issue of quality. It also contended that "failure to disclose a material aspect of the results, relating to taste, under the circumstances is misleading."

Thus, in evaluating secondary research, one must always ask whether the purpose of the study was to reach a preestablished conclusion. The researcher should then be aware of techniques used (e.g., reporting "cherry-picked" empirical results, as above) to arrive at such preordained results.

Even when the data are not collected for purposes of advocating a particular position, the purpose of the study may confound the interpretation of the data. For example, the best-known measure of price movements in the United States is the Consumer Price Index (CPI) calculated monthly by the U.S. Bureau of Labor Statistics. This index is based on the prices of about 400 items of consumption. The price of each item contributing to the index is calculated by surveying wage earners and clerical workers in some base year and computing the average price paid for each item. The index represents an average for a family of four (father, age 38; nonworking mother; boy, age 13; and girl, age 8) living in an urban area. Thus the index is not representative of the expenditures of most families. It is only a very rough index of what is happening to purchasing power and is not often useful for specific decisions where a high degree of precision is required or where expenditure patterns are different from those used to define the index.

WHO WAS RESPONSIBLE FOR COLLECTING THE INFORMATION?

Information from certain sources may be more credible than information from others. This arises not just from the biases that may be at work, but also from differences in technical competence, resources, and quality. Some organizations have developed reputations for excellent quality control work and for the integrity of their data. Others have reputations for poor work. Generally, those sources of high integrity will provide sufficient information about how the information was obtained to enable a review of the technical adequacy of the data. Learning about the reputations of various sources of information requires investigating their previous work. Contacting clients and others who have used information supplied by the organization will also provide some indication of the reputation of an organization. One might also examine the training and expertise present in an organization supplying information.

It is also worthwhile to determine whether the organization that sponsored or conducted the research had a vested interest in any particular outcome. For example, an organization that reports a study of its own effectiveness might have a vested interest in accentuating the positive. A rather sizable industry exists to produce what is often called "advocacy research." Such research is not designed to produce unbiased answers to questions. Rather, the research is conducted for the purpose of providing support for a particular conclusion or position. Although such research may still yield insights, it must be interpreted with caution.

WHAT INFORMATION
WAS ACTUALLY COLLECTED?

In the early 1950s, a congressional committee published an estimate of the annual "take" from gambling in the United States. The figure, $20 billion, actually was picked at random. One committee member was quoted as saying, "We had no real idea of the money spent. The California Crime Commission said $14 billion. Virgil Peterson of Chicago said $30 billion. We picked $20 billion as the balance of the two" (Singer, 1971, p. 410). Here is an example of information entered into the public record that had no empirical basis. No data were collected at all; only a couple of opinions were sought and averaged. "Mythical numbers," as Singer (1971) refers to them, are more common than one would wish. These mythical numbers, estimates based on pure guesswork, represent the extreme case, but they serve to emphasize the need for asking what information actually was collected.

Consider the following claim by an advertiser: "Mothers say that Brand X diapers absorb 17.5% more liquid than Brand Y." The first point to be made here is that probably no mother ever said this. Most probably, the figures are derived from a marketing research study commissioned by Brand X and averaged to arrive at this conclusion. The next point to be made is that no matter how accurately this proportion may summarize the results obtained, the data were derived from a sample of mothers. Hence sampling variation is always at issue and may be quite large if proper statistical sampling techniques were not observed. A third issue is that the statement only mentions mothers. In this day and age, fathers have been known to change a diaper or two . . . so did their opinions not count?

Taking these issues into consideration, we still must ask, what is the meaning of the advertised statement? Specifically, if Brand Y only absorbs 1 ounce of liquid, then how valuable is a diaper that can only absorb 1.175 ounces? Hence all of these criticisms leave the relevance of such an exact figure as 17.5% in doubt.

The context in which data are collected may also influence the results. Consider a study of consumer preferences that found that 60% of all consumers preferred Brand A. Such a finding is impressive until one learns that brands B and C, the major competitors of A, were not included on the list from which consumers were to select a product.

Many of the things we wish to measure cannot be observed directly. Thus we obtain an estimate indirectly by using a surrogate measure that is observable and assumed to be related to the more interesting phenomenon. The critical assumption of such indirect measurement techniques is that there is a relationship between the observable measure and the unobservable event of interest. Even when this assumption is correct, however, the relationship may be decidedly less than perfect. Consider studies of the success of graduates of corporate training programs. Success is difficult to measure because it involves a variety of dimensions and could be measured at many different points in time. One organization may report results using turnover during the year following completion of the training program. A second organization may use rapidity of advancement within the organization and salary increases during a 3-year period. Still another organization may use ratings of success by supervisors after 6 months on the job. In each case, the data may be used to relate completion of the training program to success on the job, yet the relationship reported may vary widely from one study to another. The differences in the findings are attributable to the data that actually were collected, not what these data were interpreted to mean. Knowing what information actually was obtained is often very useful for reconciling conflicting results. For example, it is well known that self-report data about behavior differ significantly from data about the incidence of the same behavior obtained by observation (Fiske, 1971).

Even when direct measurement is possible, the ways in which data are defined and classified may confound the interpretations made. Categorizations and classifications may vary widely, and their relevance and meaning for a particular purpose must always be investigated. For example, what is a family? Is a single, self-supporting person living alone a family? Are unmarried cohabitants a family? For some purposes and in some studies the answer is likely to be yes, whereas in other cases the answer is likely to be no. Wasson and Shreve (1976) provide an example of the problems caused by insufficient attention to the classification issue. For many years, the steel industry used total tonnage sold as a criterion of success. The criterion led the industry to overlook its losses of highly profitable low-tonnage sales to paper and aluminum products. Only too late did the industry recognize that a classification system based on uses and markets would have provided greater insight into events in its marketplace.

Wide variations in geographic, income, and age groupings across studies are quite common. There are often no accepted definitions for the concepts measured. Thus careful attention must be given to what information actually was obtained in a particular study. Apparent inconsistencies across studies often have more to do with the operational definition of terms than the actual differences in the underlying phenomena. Of course, such problems hinder the effective usage of meta-analysis across studies and the effective generalizability of conclusions.

The quality and relevance of information may also vary within a given source. For example, a particular data base of mental health hospitalizations was constructed for the purpose of facilitating reimbursements of expenses by such third parties as insurance companies and government agencies. Information on the length of hospitalization tended to be quite good, because this was directly relevant to the issue of reimbursement. Other information within the data base, however, was of more questionable quality. Data on discharge status were particularly poor, because they were never verified. Such data were not of central importance to the original purpose of the data base. The lesson in this example is that a source of information may be very useful for one purpose, but very poor for other purposes. Sources are not good or bad; they are useful for some purposes and not for others. The same is true for individual variables within a given source.

WHEN WAS THE INFORMATION COLLECTED?

A study of the perception of the price of long-distance telephone calls found that consumers were very much aware of the price of long-distance calls and very sensitive to even small rate hikes. The results of the study might be interpreted as an indication that consumers are very price sensitive. The study, however, was carried out while an intense, highly publicized debate over a telephone price hike raged, a debate that included several prominent politicians involved in an election campaign. It is likely that the results of the study would have been different had the study been carried out when there was less publicity about telephone rates.

Time is an important factor to be considered when evaluating information. As in the example above, factors present at the time of information collection may influence the results obtained. Time may also influence the definition of measures. For example, when is a sale made? Does the sale occur upon the placement of an order, receipt of the order, the time of shipment, the time of delivery, the date of billing, the date of payment, or the date a payment actually is recorded? Different accounting systems place emphasis on different points in time and produce differences in information. Shifts in the point of time when measurements are taken may have very pronounced effects on the results obtained.

The passage of time may also change the measurement instrument. Consider the following example provided by Wasson and Shreve (1976). In most places, the dividing line between petty and grand larceny was $50.00 in previous generations and is now $100.00. In 1910, $50.00 represented 2 months' wages, whereas today it may represent less than a day's wages. Thus it may appear that the level of crime has increased when in fact it may have been decreasing.

Time may also make information obsolete. Data on unemployment rates in the 1960s are not particularly useful for formulating policy in the 1990s. Technological changes may change perceptions; life-styles may change. Sooner or later, most secondary data become obsolete and of interest only for historical purposes. How quickly data become obsolete depends on the type of data, the purpose for which they are used, and what new data have been obtained. In the case of census data, it typically takes at least 2 years before they are published. By nature, its value quickly diminishes over time. Although periodic updates are offered by the Census Bureau itself, as well as local planning and commercial agencies, the updates generally apply to large geographic areas, so primary research may be needed to obtain data on local areas.

The user should always know when data were collected, however, particularly because there is often a substantial time lag between data collection and the publication of results. Some data remain valid despite the passage of time, of course. For example, studies of verbal learning carried out in the 1880s remain useful even today. More recent research has added to our understanding of the learning process, however, and some conclusions have been modified as new information has been obtained. For more information on the temporal boundaries of data, the interested reader should consult Kelly and McGrath (1988) in this series.

HOW WAS THE INFORMATION OBTAINED?

The quality of secondary data cannot be evaluated without knowledge of the methodology employed when collecting the data. Information about the size and nature of samples, response rates, experimental procedures, validation efforts, questionnaires, interview guides or protocols, and analytic methods should be available in sufficient detail to allow a knowledgeable critique of the data collection procedure. The following examples help illustrate why such information is useful.

Consider a poll that finds that 80% of the respondents in a survey opposed gun control. One's interpretation of the 80% figure would be quite different if one were to learn that the respondents were drawn from the membership roster of the National Rifle Association and not a representative sample of the total population. Suppose that a report on road accidents in Country X claimed that motorcyclists suffered a great increase in casualties during the year, based on the findings that there were 1,280 fatalities in 1990 and 1,586 in 1991 (an increase of 23.91% over the previous year). Although the data would seem to support the claim, suppose that a more penetrating examination of available information revealed that the number of registered cycles increased from 1,460,000 in 1990 to 1,910,000 in 1991 (an increase of 30.82%). Hence the rate of accidents per registered cycle, which was 0.088% in 1990, fell to 0.083% in 1991. Examination of these more complete and unreported data would lead to a different conclusion than that arrived at previously.

It has become fashionable for many periodicals to publish questionnaires for readers to complete and return. The responses are then complied and reported in the publication. Although these surveys may make entertaining reading, it is not clear to whom the results apply. How are readers of particular publications different from the general population? One would certainly expect very different responses on certain topics from readers of *Playboy* and readers of the *B'nai Brith Messenger.* It is not even reasonable to generalize such results to all readers of the magazine; the people who elected to respond may differ from those who did not. Many organizations report results of surveys of their customers or clients. Such surveys may be quite useful, but they indicate nothing about individuals or organizations that are not customers or clients.

The question of sampling and sample design—how people are selected for participation in a survey—is a critical issue for the evaluation of data because it deals with the question of generalizability of results. It is also important to determine who responded and the response rate.

A survey with a response rate of 80% is certainly more credible than one with a 5% response rate. Given that a result was obtained from a particular study, can that result be considered representative of some larger population? What is the nature of that population? All too frequently one finds that it is impossible to identify that larger population.

A description of the sampling procedure is always necessary when evaluating the usefulness of data. For example, suppose that it was reported by an independent research firm that 60% of subjects given a test drive of both a Honda Civic and a Ford Escort chose the latter on the basis of overall quality. This result is impressive for Ford but becomes questionable if it is determined that all of those sampled lived in Detroit and, furthermore, that all of the individuals worked for Ford. The sampling issue applies not only to people but also to other units, such as time, organizations, locations, and situations. A more detailed description of survey and sampling procedures may be found in two companion volumes of this series (Fowler, 1988; Henry, 1991).

A chronic problem with much research in the social sciences is that of missing data. Data may be missing for a variety of reasons, but the most frequent is nonresponse. When obtaining information from people, it is impossible to obtain data from everyone of interest. Individuals may not be found, or they may simply refuse to cooperate. Even the Census Bureau, which is charged with collecting information about the whole population, fails to obtain 100% response rates. Obviously a 95% response rate is good, and a 5% response rate is poor, but there are no clear guidelines for discounting information as a result of a low response rate. The issue of response rate applies to both the level of the observation and the variables within an observation. For example, a survey might produce a very high response rate, but a particular item in the survey may have been left unanswered by 60% of the respondents. Such an item would need to be interpreted with caution if it were used at all.

It is often helpful to know the reasons for nonresponse when evaluating information. It is also useful to compare respondents with nonrespondents on whatever information may be available for such purposes. Some information about demographic characteristics is generally obtainable, and comparisons of respondents and nonrespondents should be reported for these characteristics.

Sampling and response rates are not the only details of the data collection procedure that should be available. Copies of measurement instruments, questionnaires, coding forms, and the like help to identify what information actually was obtained, how it was obtained, and the validity of the inferences made from the data.

A common means for summarizing information about trends is the use of percentages. A large proportion of government data, as well as data from other sources, is presented in percentage form. Though this may be useful in some cases, it can also be misleading. Percentages are relative. A 10% change is quite different when the base is 100 than when it is 1,000,000. Large percentage changes often arise when computations are based on small numbers. Managers often do not understand why last year's 400% increase in sales has dropped to a 50% increase in the current year. The reason may be simply one of an increasing base on which the percentage figure is calculated. Thus percentages are seldom particularly useful unless one has knowledge of their base.

A frequent method for summarizing differences among groups involves a transformation of percentages. This transformation produces an index number. Index numbers may be calculated in many ways, but all involve a comparison of two percentages. For example, assume that 20% of the population as a whole owns a personal computer. Among engineers, 80% own a personal computer, but only 20% of architects own one. Indices representing the likelihood of ownership of a personal computer by occupation may be constructed by dividing the percentage of ownership for each group by the percentage of ownership for the population as a whole, as follows:

$$\text{Index for engineers} = 80\%/20\% \times 100 = 400$$
$$\text{Index for architects} = 20\%/20\% \times 100 = 100$$

These numbers would be interpreted to mean that the engineers as a group are four times as likely as the general population to own personal computers, whereas architects are just as likely as the general population to own personal computers. Such indices are very useful when one is trying to present information about many groups, but note that the index is the ratio of two relative measures. Thus very high (or very low) indices may reflect small or large bases for computation. In addition, each percentage used in the computation is itself an estimate. Consequently, the error present in an index is a combination of the errors present in the two percentages used in the computation.

Another example that illustrates how important it is to reflect upon the base of an index can be shown in the construction of a price index. For simplicity, consider the following consumer price index based upon two products: Brand W water and Brand Y yogurt. Assume that the prices of Brand W and Brand Y are recorded as follows:

	1991 Price	1992 Price
Brand W	$1.50/bottle	$3.00/bottle
Brand Y	$3.00/6-pack	$1.50/6-pack

These data show that Brand W in 1992 was twice as expensive as it was in 1991, whereas Brand Y was half as expensive. Assume now that two different researchers have been asked to take these data and to construct a price index. Researcher A decides to use 1991 as the base and comes up with the following calculations:

	1991	1992
Brand W	100	200
(relative to base)		
Brand Y	100	50
(relative to base)		
Total	200	250
Combined index	100	125

Researcher A, using the combined index above (which is the arithmetic average of levels for the two individual brands) shows that, on average, prices rose 25%. Meanwhile, Researcher B decides to use 1992 as the base and arrives at the following calculations.

	1991	1992
Brand W	50	100
(relative to base)		
Brand Y	200	100
(relative to base)		
Total	250	200
Combined index	125	100

From the results above, Researcher B concludes that prices, on average, decreased by 25%. It is interesting to note that both researchers worked with identical data, yet arrived at dramatically different conclusions. By simply changing the base year, prices were made to appear to go up as opposed to going down.

Now Researcher C comes along and proclaims that both of the other two researchers are incorrect. He states that it is obvious that if one were to buy a bottle of Brand W and a six-pack of Brand Y in either year, the cost ($4.50) would be identical. That is, there has been no change in the total at all. Now an individual who relies upon a logical conclusion from these data can proclaim that prices have risen, declined, or remained the same, depending upon the choice of researcher! Of course, the fallacy in all of this is that the percentage relatives within Brands W and Y are not percentages based upon the same quantity. A 100% increase in the price of Brand W would represent $1.50, whereas the same percentage increase in Brand Y prices would represent $3.00. For an effective index to be constructed, the respective percentage changes must first be weighted in proportion to their relative base prices. The weighted percentages thus are expressed to a common base (e.g., 1991) and can now be combined mathematically for averaging purposes as follows:

	1991	1992	% Relative	Weight	Product
Brand W	$1.50	$3.00	200	1	200
Brand Y	$3.00	$1.50	50	2	100
			Totals	3	300

The average product in the example above is 100, which represents the combined index number. Hence support for the conclusion of Researcher C is found, as prices have indeed remained unchanged. Sometimes when data are transformed, the transformations themselves are transformed. In fact, an index is really a transformation of a transformation—first raw data are changed to percentages, and then a ratio of percentages is obtained. It is important to understand what specific transformations have been performed and how these transformations were done. The lesson to be learned from all of this is that one must always question the ways in which conclusions are derived in the interpretation and usage of secondary information.

Similarly, any experimental or field procedure should also be described in detail. For example, in a study of consumer reactions to a new product, it would be useful to know whether the product actually was used by the consumers or whether it simply was described to them. Reports on the technical performance of products should specify the conditions under which measures were obtained. The automobile mileage estimates disseminated by the Environmental Protection Agency are obtained under conditions quite different from those under which most automobiles operate.

When evaluating the procedures employed in collecting information, the crucial question is one of bias. Was something done (or not done) in the study that would lead to a particular result, produce results that may not be generalizable, or confound the interpretation of results? Such information is not always available. When it is available, a more useful assessment of the data provided can be done. When it is not, a healthy skepticism is in order.

Finally, evaluation of how data were obtained should include attention to the quality of the data themselves. Is there evidence that the measures were reliable, valid, and complete? Some measures may be very ad hoc, whereas others may be based on careful development and application over long periods of time. Some measures may reflect only a portion of the data of interest. For example, electronic scanner data may reflect the purchases of a household in a supermarket, but miss any purchases of similar products that might be purchased in a discount store or other outlet.

HOW CONSISTENT IS THE INFORMATION WITH OTHER INFORMATION?

When data are presented by multiple independent sources, one's confidence in those data is increased. Given all of the problems that may be present in secondary data and the frequent difficulty with identifying how the data were obtained, the best strategy is to find multiple sources of information. Ideally, two or more independent sources should arrive at the same or similar conclusions. When disagreement among sources does exist, it is helpful to try to identify reasons for such differences and to determine which source is more credible. This is not always easy, even with relatively complete information. When radically different results are reported and little basis for evaluating the information collection procedure is found, it is appropriate to be skeptical of all of the data.

A NOTE ON THE INTERPRETATION OF NUMBERS

Secondary data often come in the form of numbers. Numerical data have the appearance of being "hard" data, tangible and concrete, when compared to information presented in words. Yet a number is the ultimate abstraction, with no inherent meaning. Numbers are simply vehicles for carrying information. The user of secondary data should be comfortable with numerical data, but should also understand that numbers are no better than the information they represent and the process by which that information was generated. Unfortunately, many secondary sources do not provide the most useful numerical information, as the examples above in terms of indexes revealed.

Other descriptive statistics can also pose problems. Means are seldom useful without accompanying information. Generally, one would also like to have an indication of the variability of the sample or population and the number of observations on which the mean was computed. Such information facilitates the identification of significant differences, gives a better perspective on the underlying form of the data, and (other things being equal) improves the confidence one places in the data.

As an example, consider the table below, which shows the profit and losses (as a percentage of sales) of a company's six divisions for the years 1991 and 1992:

Division	1991	1992
A	+28%	−2%
B	−15%	+60%
C	+2%	−5%
D	−12%	+20%
E	+26%	−14%
F	+19%	−11%
Totals	+48%	+48%
Mean	+8%	+8%

Reporting from the above data that the average profitability across divisions for the company is the same for the 2 years is problematic for two reasons. First, the percentage increases (or decreases) reported by each division cloak the fact the some divisions had greater sales than others, and hence these divisions should be weighted more strongly in the mean calculation. Second, although the means are the same, there has been a dramatic shift between divisions in terms of profitability. That is, each division that was profitable in 1991 was not profitable in 1992, and vice versa. This example again illustrates the difficulty in relying on reported secondary summary statistics without knowledge of the data used in their construction.

SUMMARY

All data are not created equal. When using secondary sources, it is important to evaluate very carefully the information presented, to weigh potential biases, and to adopt an attitude of healthy skepticism. Conclusions should not be accepted at face value simply because they are in print, or because the claim is made that they are based on empirical research. Evidence in support of conclusions must be evaluated and weighed carefully to determine whether such conclusions are justified. Alternative explanations for research findings should be identified and considered. Factors other than those identified in the study may have produced a particular result. Only careful consideration of the methods employed to collect and analyze the data will reveal such alternative explanations. Confidence in the conclusions of one study is bolstered when these conclusions also are supported in other studies. The use of multiple sources of information is, ultimately, the best defense against being misled.

EXERCISES

Exercise 2.1: The Consumer Price Index was referred to above. Reread the description of the CPI. Until recently, one assumption of the CPI was that the family of four for which the CPI is representative would purchase a new home each month. What biases are introduced by such an assumption? Who would have a vested interest in maintaining such an assumption?

Exercise 2.2: A report on university students' sexual practices was published in a well-known magazine. The data were obtained from questionnaires sent in by readers of the publication. How useful are the results of the survey? What problems with this study might lead you to question the findings?

Exercise 2.3: During a municipal campaign for passage of a tax referendum, proponents of the tax increase obtained information on the tax rates of other municipalities. The conclusion drawn from these data was that, of 12 municipalities of comparable size, 11 had higher tax rates than the one in which the referendum was held. What questions might you ask about the conclusion drawn and the data used to support this conclusion?

Exercise 2.4: A manufacturer of appliances developed an advertising campaign that emphasized the results of a survey of appliance repair personnel. The results indicated that the manufacturer's products were regarded as the most reliable of all such products. Only repair personnel who serviced more than one brand of appliance, however, were included in the survey. What questions might be raised about the study cited by the advertising?

Exercise 2.5: Several firms provide information to their subscribers about the movement of grocery products. Some firms monitor a sample of warehouses and obtain information on warehouse shipments to retailers. Others audit a sample of retail stores. Still others collect scanner checkout data where optical scanners are in use. How might these three methods of collecting data on sales volume lead to differing conclusions.

3

Government Information, Part I: Census Data

The U.S. government carries out 11 censuses on a regular basis. Data from these studies are valuable for a wide range of applications. Census information is available on households, businesses, government units, transportation, and natural resources. The Census Bureau provides considerable assistance for learning about and accessing census data. This chapter offers an introduction to census data and their use.

The government of the United States is the world's largest gatherer of information. This "official" information generally is obtained as a by-product of administrative and regulatory functions. Such information may take the form of either censuses or specifically commissioned studies of rather specific subjects. So great is the amount of information generated by the federal government that a single directory or guide is unavailable.

In terms of census information, perhaps the most useful introduction to the information resources of the government is the *Census Catalog and Guide*. This publication describes all Census Bureau products, including reports, computer tapes, microcomputer diskettes, CD-ROM availability, microfiche, and maps issued from mid-1988 through December 1989. It also includes a section on statistical publications from other federal agencies, indexes, and a directory of more than 3,000 sources of assistance, such as 200 specialists at the Census Bureau and 1,400 state data center organizations. Regarding statistical data published by the government, the *Statistical Abstract of the United States* is most comprehensive. This publication of the Department of Commerce is available from the U.S. Government Printing Office and is a guide and summary of statistics on the social, political, and economic status of government and business in the United States. Other publications that provide useful introductions to government information are listed in Table 3.1.

The federal government is not the only government producing information. State and local governments also produce substantial amounts of information, as do foreign governments and international organizations. Such information ranges from statistics on road use to attitudes

Table 3.1

Publications Providing Introduction to Federal Statistics

American Statistics Index: A Comprehensive Guide and Index to the Statistical Publications of the U.S. Government

Published on a monthly basis since 1973, with annual cumulations. It represents a guide to publications and data available from the federal government. Compiled by the Congressional Information Service.

Census Catalog and Guide (1990)

This publication describes all Census Bureau products, including reports, computer tapes, microcomputer diskettes, CD-ROM, microfiche, and maps, issued from mid-1988 through December 1989. It also includes plans for 1990 census products, a new section on statistical publications from other federal agencies, indexes, and a directory of more than 3,000 sources of assistance, such as 200 specialists at the Census Bureau and 1,400 state data center organizations. The catalog is updated by a monthly U.S. Census Bureau publication called *Census and You.*

Guide to Foreign Trade Statistics

Published by the Bureau of the Census and issued periodically, this guide to foreign trade statistics provides a description of U.S. Census Bureau publications dealing with foreign trade, as well as sample tables.

Historical Statistics of the United States: Colonial Times to 1970

Contains annual data on 3,000 different statistical series concerning economic, social, and political life in the United States since colonial times. Consistent definitions of variables are used throughout, thus facilitating comparisons across time.

Statistical Abstract of the United States

A convenient statistical reference and directory to more detailed statistics reported in a variety of other government publications. Reproduces more than 1,000 tables published in other Census Bureau publications and provides a table of footnotes and a bibliography of sources. Provides new tables relating to marital status, health insurance information, government and economic activities, and wood energy consumption, among others. Also includes a pocket-sized insert titled "USA Statistics in Brief" that summarizes important data for quick and easy reference. Note that definitions of certain categories have changed over time, making it difficult to do comparisons over time. For such analyses, the Census Bureau has published a special sourcebook that is described below.

Statistics Sources (1989)

Designed as a user's guide to statistical sources, this document provides descriptions of both government and nongovernment data sources. Focuses on business, industrial, financial, and social among other disciplines.

of the general public regarding sex education. In the remainder of this chapter, data produced by one federal agency, the Bureau of the Census, will be examined; analogous data produced by international organizations will be discussed as well. Chapter 4 will examine other types of government information.

THE BUREAU OF THE CENSUS

The Census Bureau has its origins in the U.S. Constitution, which mandates a census as the basis for apportioning representation in the U.S. House of Representatives. The earliest censuses were little more than counts of people, but over the years more and more information has been collected. Census data tend to be of very high quality and are available at a sufficient level of detail to be useful for many purposes. In fact, there are multiple censuses today, not just one. These collect a wide range of information that is far removed from the simple "head count" mandated in the Constitution. Table 3.2 provides a description of the 11 censuses carried out by the bureau. The Census Bureau produces detailed summaries of the information it obtains and, for a fee, will provide data on CD-ROM or magnetic tape. For example, the 1987 economic census (including the censuses of retail trade, wholesale trade, service industries, manufacturers, mineral industries, construction industries, and transportation) and the 1987 census of agriculture were made available on CD-ROM in 1991. The bureau also sells computer software that may be used for accessing and tabulating data.

The quality of data obtained by the Census Bureau is, in part, a reflection of both the professional expertise within the bureau and the political pressures that are brought to bear on it. The bureau employs many highly skilled social scientists who design and execute each census. The actual data collection is carried out by mail and by paid census takers who have been trained carefully to collect information. Although not everyone responds to the census, considerable effort is made to recontact nonrespondents in order to obtain information. For example, the Census Bureau estimated that it actually contacted 98% of the population during the 1990 census. In recent years, census data have taken on added importance, because the federal government often allocates funds to state and local governments based on these data. Lawsuits have on occasion been filed by state and local governments because they—for whatever reason—believed that the census data represented a biased count of persons. As a result of such lawsuits, as well as general political pressures, the bureau attempts to maintain a high-quality data collection effort that can withstand very careful scrutiny.

Although the amount of data obtained by the bureau is impressive, it is not without its drawbacks. The very size of the data collection effort, editing, coding, tabulation, and verification delay the availability of the data. As an example, the earliest results for the 1990 population census

Text continued on page 38

Table 3.2

Regularly Conducted Censuses of the Bureau of the Census

Decennial Census of Population

The census of population is taken every 10 years, in years ending in zero. The most recent census was taken in 1990. The census reports the population for states, counties, all incorporated population centers, minor civil divisions, standard metropolitan areas, and unincorporated land populated by 1,000 or more individuals. It also provides a detailed description of subpopulations on such characteristics as sex, marital status, age, race, ethnic origin, education, family size, and relationship to the head of the household. General social and economic characteristics such as mobility, state and nation of birth, number and composition of families, employment status, occupation, and income are also reported. In addition, special reports on population and housing by census tract are provided. *Current Population Reports,* published annually, updates the information in the census of population based on the latest information on birthrates and death rates, migration, and so on. Preliminary information from this census reveals that the U.S. population has increased over the past 10 years by approximately 10% to 249,632,692, with the greatest percentage increases in the 30-44 age bracket and the 75-and-older age group. In addition, the Sun Belt region of the United States appears to have had the greatest increase in population, with California, Florida, and Texas showing the greatest percentage gain. In terms of race, the greatest growth appears to be evidenced by persons of Asian origin.

Decennial Census of Housing

Data on housing are collected simultaneously with the population census. Information is provided about such characteristics as building condition, type of structure, number of occupants, number of rooms, value, monthly mortgage or rent payment, water and sewage facilities, and equipment such as air conditioners, stoves, and dishwashers. For large metropolitan areas and certain other geographic units, data are provided at the city-block level. *Current Housing Reports* is an annual update of the census of housing.

Census of Agriculture

Provides a statistical picture of agriculture in the United States on the national, state, and local levels. Separate volumes are issued for each state, the District of Columbia, Guam, Puerto Rico, and the Virgin Islands, as well as a United States summary. The state volumes contain county as well as aggregate data for the state. All farming, ranching, and related activities are included. Each census is compared with the previous census. Beginning with 1982, the census is now taken every 5 years, in years ending with a 2 or 7; hence 1992 was the most recent.

Census of Retail Trade

Part of the economic census. This effort is multivolume in form and presents detailed statistics on all businesses engaged in selling merchandise for personal or household consumption. The three major volumes are as follows: Volume 1 presents retail summary and industry statistics, including information on establishment and firm size, measures of value produced and capital expenditures, and so forth. Volume 2 presents geographic area statistics for retail trade, including statistics for each state, standard metropolitan statistical area (SMSA), county, and places with a population of 2,500 or more. Finally, Volume 3 presents information on major retail centers, including statistics for central business districts and major retail centers in each SMSA. All statistics are presented by kind of business (according to SIC codes) for each topic or geographic area.

Table 3.2 Continued

This census is published every 5 years, in years ending in a 2 or a 7; hence the most recent census was in 1992.

Census of Wholesale Trade
Part of the economic census. This census contains data on wholesale establishments, with payrolls, that are engaged primarily in selling merchandise to retailers; to industrial, commercial, institutional, farm, or professional users; or to other wholesalers, excluding government organizations. Presented in two volumes, the first volume deals with industry statistics and the second with geographic area statistics. Data are presented by kind of business (SIC) for each topic or geographic area, with statistics on the number of establishments, sales, payroll, number of employees and type of operation, and so forth. Industry statistics include establishment and firm size, measures of value produced, capital expenditures, depreciable assets, and operating expenses.

Census of Selected Service Industries
Part of the economic census. A geographic series consisting of 52 separate reports makes up the first and largest section of this census. Both taxed and tax-exempt enterprises are covered, arranged by kind of business. Data are given for the United States as a whole, individual states and the District of Columbia, counties, and places with either 2,500 inhabitants or 300 or more establishments. Number of establishments, receipts, payroll, and number of employees are given in every case. The census is published in years ending with a 2 or 7, with the most recent census taken in 1992.

Census of Selected Construction Industries
Part of the economic census. Provides a detailed analysis of all construction establishments with a payroll. These establishments primarily engage in contract construction, developing, or land subdividing. The detailed analysis included the number of establishments, payroll, assets, and type of construction. The data are further divided into industry, states, and SMSAs.

Census of Governments
Data are obtained on the number of governmental units by state, county, and city, as well as information on government employment, elected officials, finances, taxable property values, amount of indebtedness, operating revenues and costs, and payroll. This census is taken in years ending with a 2 or a 7; the most recent census was taken in 1992.

Census of Manufacturers
Part of the economic census. Statistics are provided on size of establishments, forms of organization, products shipped and consumed, payrolls, employment, inventories, capital expenditures, value added by the manufacturer, and consumption of fuel, water, and energy. Manufacturers are categorized by type, using the approximately 450 classes in the Standard Industrial Classification System (SIC). Information is summarized by SIC code and by geographic region. The *Annual Survey of Manufacturers* provides an update of the census. Monthly and annual production figures for certain commodities are contained in *Current Industrial Reports*. This census is published in years ending in a 2 or a 7; the most recent census was in 1992.

Census of Mineral Industries
Data are obtained by state and nine geographic regions on size and number of mining establishments, employment, payrolls, power and water use, equipment use, production, value of shipments, capital expenditures, type of organization, use and cost of selected supplies, and fuel and electrical energy needs. This census is comparable to

(Continued)

Table 3.2 Continued

the census of manufacturers but is particular to the mining industry. Data are broken down for some 50 categories of industries, using SIC codes. The Bureau of Mines of the Department of the Interior updates these data annually; however, the data are aggregated by product rather than by industrial classification. This census is taken in the years ending in a 2 or a 7; the most recent census was taken in 1992.

Census of Transportation

Part of the economic census. There are four major components of this census: the Commodity Transport Survey, the Passenger Transport Survey, the Truck Inventory and Use Survey, and the Bus and Truck Carrier Survey. The travel information provided includes purpose, duration, origin and destination, size of party, lodgings used, and socioeconomic characteristics of travelers. The census is taken in years ending in either a 2 or a 7; the most recent census was taken in 1992.

SOURCE: Adapted from Priscilla Geahigoin and Robert Rose (1988), *Business Serials of the U.S. Government,* 2nd ed. (ALA Publishers).

were not available until the middle of 1991, and detailed results were not available until 1992. Indeed, it is not unusual for data to be 2 or more years old before they are available in report or computer-accessible form. Further compounding this time lag between data collection and the availability of results is the fact that the censuses are not annual; they are taken every fifth or tenth year. Thus it is possible in some cases for the latest census data available to be as much as 12 years old.

A second drawback of census data is that, like all secondary data, they are not always in the form most useful for the purpose at hand. This is particularly true when data are obtained from tabulation reports of the bureau rather than from a customized analysis of the data. Definitions of categories may not be the most appropriate for a particular use, and standard reports by geographic units are not always the most helpful approach for many analyses. This problem may be remedied somewhat by CD-ROM, which allows users (with limitations) to undertake customized analyses of the data.

ACCESSING CENSUS DATA

The very size of the census poses problems for the researcher. The Census Bureau publishes so much information that it has become necessary for it to provide assistance to users. There are a number of very useful guides to the census data. The Census Bureau's *Census Catalog and*

Guide describes special studies and provides interim estimates; this document is published annually but is updated monthly by *Census and You,* which gives up-to-date information about bureau programs, products, and services and the latest news about demographic and economic data. Also available are the *Index to Selected 1990 Census Reports* and the *Index to 1990 Census Summary Tapes,* which provide a list of all tables available from the 1990 population census by form, variables reported, and level of aggregation.

Every major metropolitan area has at least one regional depository of federal government documents, as do many smaller cities. This may be a university library or a public library. Census publications, including those identified above, are available at these depositories. In addition, selected Census Bureau publications can be purchased through the Government Printing Office. The government also makes available a list of products on CD-ROM that can be purchased through the mail. Such products include the 1987 economic censuses, the 1987 census of agriculture, and TIGER/Line final postcensus files for 1990 (see below). In addition, the Bureau of the Census provides a free newsletter titled "Data Developments" that keeps the user up to date with any developments on the data front (including new data available on CD-ROM).

The availability of the 1990 census on CD-ROM and the introduction of the Topologically Integrated Geographic Coding and Referencing (TIGER) system are the two major innovations for the 1990 population census. The TIGER system gives the user the ability to generate a digitized street map of the entire 3.6 million-square-mile map of the United States. Specifically, with use of the TIGER system, one can literally chart every block in every county in the United States, both topographically and demographically.

Although TIGER originally was developed for use by the Census Bureau to manage the 1990 census effectively by linking addresses to specific blocks, other uses have evolved naturally. Businesses and other organizations are now able to use TIGER to define the geographic boundaries of their customers more accurately and hence can allocate fixed resources more optimally. Those organizations that may benefit most from TIGER are direct marketers or those who focus on delivery. For example, TIGER will give direct marketers the ability to pinpoint customer addresses, with the subsequent ability to cluster them for segmentation purposes. Similarly, any company involved in home delivery will find TIGER useful in locating customer destinations.

TIGER is not, however, limited to only business applications. For instance, using a TIGER-based geographic information system, the health department of a major state can code its cancer patients' addresses and then access 1990 census population data to determine the cancer incidence rates for specific geographic areas. A major city might use a TIGER-derived street network as part of a project to identify traffic patterns and industrial polluters. As a case in point, the roar of TIGER was heard following the Loma Prieta, California, earthquake of 1989. After the quake, the U.S. Army Corps of Engineers realized that they did not have on hand a uniform map data base for the quake-prone northern California area. They made an urgent call to the Census Bureau for an advance copy of TIGER/Line files for the area. The request was granted, and within 24 hours the TIGER/Line data had been translated into another digital format and converted into a single consistent computer map for the entire earthquake-affected zone. This enabled Federal Emergency Management Agency officials to locate damage reports quickly and to determine the status of emergency response operations. Two days after the initial request, the Army Corps of Engineers had TIGER-based sheet maps in the hands of their field inspectors.

As the Bureau of the Census notes, "Like any new product as complex as a digital map base for the entire country, TIGER has engendered its share of myths about what it is and how it works" (U.S. Bureau of Census, 1990, p. 9); some of the most popular are indicated in Table 3.3. Five versions of the TIGER maps are available from the government. These include the prototype and precensus versions, both issued in 1989; the Initial Voting District Codes (VTD) version released in October of 1990, which blankets the United States by election districts; and the initial and final postcensus versions, the latter released in the early part of 1991. TIGER covers 3,286 counties in the United States, including addresses from the most populated urban areas to the most rural areas.

Because many organizations, both commercial and nonprofit, make extensive use of census data for planning purposes, the Industry and Trade Administration has published *Measuring Markets: A Guide to the Use of Federal and State Statistical Data* (1979). This extremely readable and useful publication explains how census data may be applied to solve a variety of problems. *Measuring Markets* provides an overview of census data, a number of very good illustrations of how the data may be applied to specific problems, and a bibliography of additional references and data available from individual states. Two of the case illustrations in the publication are reprinted at the end of this chapter: One concerns a location problem for a new playground; the other concerns a problem of estimating demand for a product. These illustrations provide insight

Table 3.3
Information About TIGER

Myth No. 1: TIGER is just one big map; load it into your computer and see a street map pop up on your monitor screen.

Reality: TIGER is a digital data base that allows a user to integrate map features topologically with other data (demographic, economic, etc.) by means of suitable applications software. Display a TIGER/Line record and what you will see are strings of codes. Software is what enables you to use TIGER to generate different kinds of lists and maps. The Census Bureau does not provide the software; it must be developed or purchased from a software developer. The Census Bureau will supply a list of software vendors upon request.

Myth No. 2: TIGER contains both geographic and census data.

Reality: TIGER extracts contain exclusively a digital description of geographic areas, including political and statistical area boundaries and codes, latitude/longitude coordinates, feature names and types, and (mostly in metropolitan areas) address ranges. They currently do not contain any census data. The data can be obtained separately and added to the digital map data base with appropriate software.

Myth No. 3: TIGER gives you building-by-building street addresses.

Reality: Disclosure of individual census information, including individual addresses, is prohibited under Title 13, U.S. Code. For that reason, the Census Bureau provides only address ranges for street segments. Even these ranges may require considerable user updating in many areas.

Myth No. 4: TIGER comes on one easy-to-use tape (or CD-ROM).

Reality: Precensus TIGER/Line files take up about 125 high-density computer tapes (or 38 CD-ROM diskettes). The size of all the precensus TIGER/Line files for the United States, Puerto Rico, the Virgin Islands, and the outlying areas of the Pacific is more than 20,000 megabytes. The initial Voting District Codes version of the TIGER/Line files is about 24,000 megabytes.

Source: *TIGER: The Coast-to-Coast Digital Map Data Base,* U.S. Bureau of the Census (November 1990).

into some of the types of data available from the Census Bureau and how these data may be used for solving practical problems.

Census data are available at various levels of aggregation ranging from the smallest unit, a city block, to the entire nation. A *city block* generally is defined as a geographic unit bounded by four streets, but some other physical boundary (e.g., a river) may also be involved. Blocks are aggregated arbitrarily to form *block groups,* which in turn are aggregated to form *census tracts.* Figure 3.1 illustrates the relationship among these units of analysis. Tracts usually are defined by local communities and often, but not always, provide approximations for neighborhoods. Cen-

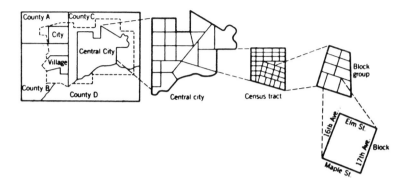

Figure 3.1. Levels of Aggregation of the Population Census

sus tract data may be aggregated to obtain information at the county, city, or state level.

Written reports of census data are not available at every level of aggregation. Data tapes or CD-ROM files must be used in such cases, and special tabulations performed. A number of private firms will provide such special tabulations if the user prefers not to purchase data files and the appropriate software to access them. A number of these firms, and the services they offer, are identified in Chapter 5.

Currently, CD-ROM software designed to access census data is available from the Institute for Electronic Data Analysis in Knoxville, Tennessee. An example of such software, SHIP, supports county and city agricultural and population statistics, county income and employment, or business indicators. The program is completely menu driven, requiring no special training or previous computer experience. It allows for custom analysis of data by locating user-specified data items from the selected records and then displaying them in tables in the order specified by the user. The program labels columns and displays tables on the screen, prints them, or stores them on magnetic disk for future use, and finally transfers user-selected data to comma-deleted magnetic disk files for use with spreadsheets, statistical packages, and other programs. The 1990 population census data are also available on the bureau's on-line data base, CENDATA, which is accessible through DIALOG Information Services and various other on-line information services, such as CompuServe and GEnie.

One relatively recent innovative use of census data has combined the demographic census data with block groups, census tracts, and zip codes in a new form of analysis called *geodemographics*. One such system, called Potential Rating Index Zip Markets (PRIZM) and created by Claritas Corporation, helps target consumer segments by describing each neighborhood in the United States in terms of 12 social groups with subsets of 40 distinct cluster types that are very homogeneous within themselves and quite distinct from other groups with respect to demographic characteristics. The underlying assumption is that people who are similar tend to live near one another. For example, one of the 40 clusters includes primarily blue-collar workers over the age of 50 with high incomes. A second group consists of areas with many high-income families containing one or more small children. The usefulness of this approach may be seen in its use by a university development office. By cross-referencing its alumni list with PRIZM areas, it was able to identify older, high-income alumni at the block level. Mailings soliciting particular types of donations to the university were directed at these individuals, making each mailing more efficient and better suited to its audience. Another use of these data would be to use the zip codes on completed product warranty cards to create profiles of purchasers.

PRIZM data, which can be linked to a wide array of syndicated data, are based on key census variables plus more than 100 million purchase records. The newest innovation, PRIZM + 4, was built up from individual household data and provides PRIZM data for 9-digit zip code areas that average 12 households. This allows the researcher greater flexibility to target specific households in terms of marketing strategy. A very readable and entertaining discussion of PRIZM is provided by Weiss (1988) in his book *The Clustering of America*.

WHAT TO DO WHILE YOU WAIT
FOR THE NEXT CENSUS

As noted in the beginning of this chapter, a problem with the census is that it often takes 2 years for a full reporting of the data. Hence researchers at times are reduced to working with numbers that can be rather old. This is problematic and emphasizes the need to estimate current populations. According to Raymondo (1989), there are five common ways to estimate a population: the censal ratio method, the housing unit method, component method II, the administrative-records method, and the ratio-correlation method.

Censal Ratio Method

This technique involves the researcher updating a population through the use of related surrogate variables whose change over the time period of interest is known. Variables that are linked to population change are the population birthrate, death rate, motor vehicle registrations, and school enrollments. So assume that a researcher decided to use the increase in motor vehicle registrations in estimating the 1990 population for City A, which had a population of 10,000 in 1980. If this measure increased by 15% during the 10-year period, then an estimate for the population of the city would be $10,000 + (10,000 \times 0.15)$, or 11,500. Of course, more than one surrogate measure could be used, which in the most simple scenario would require an averaging of their proportional changes.

The main advantage of this technique is that it is a simple calculation based on typically available data. The primary disadvantage is that accuracy declines as a function of time since the original data were collected. It also makes strong assumptions about the relationship between the surrogate variable and the population. For example, the population of a given area could grow rapidly even if the number of motor vehicle registrations remained stable. This could happen if the reason for the increase in population was an increase in the birthrate rather than people moving into a community. This makes the choice of the surrogate measure a critical element in the successful application of the censal ratio approach.

Housing Unit Method

This method requires the use of three separate component series to arrive at an estimate of the residential population: (a) the number of occupied housing units, (b) the average household size, and (c) the group-quarters population (people who live in nursing homes, jails, dorms, etc.). If one were to multiply the estimated number of occupied housing units by the average household size and then add in the group-quarters population, the result is an estimate of the total population. Estimates of the current housing stock can be arrived at through an examination of building and demolition permits. Utility service connections and disconnections can be a guide to estimating the occupancy rate. Household size can be obtained from the prior census, with the caveat that it does change over time. The main advantage of this technique is that it also involves a simple calculation that is not dependent on old data. The main disadvantage is that the estimate is only as good as the quality of the data that make up its component parts. Data requirements are demanding.

Component Method II and the Administrative-Records Method

Both of these methods divide population change into three separate components: births, deaths, and migration. Hence the current population is equal to the prior population at the time of the census plus these three components. Birth and death statistics are available at the county level and for some cities. Migration figures must be estimated on the basis of other indicators, and in how this is done lies the distinction between these methods. Component Method II (developed by the Census Bureau) uses elementary school enrollment as a proxy for migration for the population younger than 65, whereas the administrative-records method uses federal tax returns. For the population 65 or older, both techniques use Medicare records. The main advantage of both techniques is that they account for individual components of population change. The main disadvantage is that tax records may be difficult to obtain; whereas basing migration on school enrollment may be problematic.

Ratio-Correlation Method

This technique uses multiple regression to derive a predictive equation of population as a function of a series of independent predictor variables. Predictor variables typically include births, deaths, school enrollments, and voter registrations. The equation in simple form takes the form of Y (population) $= a + b(X)$, where X represents a predictor variable such as birthrate. When multiple X variables are present, a multiple regression equation is created. The main advantage of this technique is that it is flexible and can be used with many independent variables. The main disadvantage is that the equation is only as effective as the quality of the data that are input.

The question always surfaces as to which of these techniques is best. The answer is to use the technique for which you have the highest-quality data. Although the Census Bureau bases its estimates on an average of three of these methods, most businesses and academic institutions do not have the resources or the access to data to undertake such an effort. Fortunately, the Census Bureau makes its estimates available to the public in the P-25 and P-26 series of *Current Population Reports,* which provide the results of the most recent population estimates and projections produced by the Bureau.

THE STANDARD INDUSTRIAL
CLASSIFICATION SYSTEM

The Bureau of the Census has developed a uniform system of numbers for classifying organizations on the basis of their economic activities. This system is called the Standard Industrial Classification System (SIC) of codes, and it is the key to using census data related to economics, manufacturing, mining, and business. The classification system is recognized widely and has been incorporated into a variety of other government and proprietary information. A listing of code numbers may be found in the *Standard Industrial Classification Manual* (1990) published by the U.S. Office of Management and Budget.

The U.S. economy is divided into 11 major areas, such as forestry, fisheries, and manufacturing. These major divisions are categorized into industry groups identified by two-digit codes. For example, SIC 25 encompasses furniture and fixtures. Subgroups of industries are identified by a third single-digit code; hence the three-digit code 252 includes firms that manufacture office furniture. A fourth number refers to specific industries, so that the code 2522 represents metal office furniture. Up to three additional digits may be used to identify specific products, making the SIC code up to seven digits in length. This detailed a classification is not found in the *Standard Industrial Classification Manual* but is available in other reference works, such as the *U.S. Census of Manufacturers.* Every firm or plant is given an SIC code that best describes the primary activity at its location. Thus it is extremely important to be able to identify the correct SIC code when searching for secondary sources about an industry, because many standard business directories, periodical indexes, and statistical compilations make reference to them.

Numerous organizations that provide information about industries use SIC categories. Several of these are discussed in Chapter 5. The Bureau of the Census publishes *U.S. Industrial Outlook* and *County Business Patterns,* which provide summaries and updates of information. The former publication, published annually, provides descriptions and 5-year forecasts for more than 350 service and manufacturing industries. The latter provides a series of annual reports containing data on detailed economic activity at the county level for the United States overall, the 50 states, and the District of Columbia.

One particularly useful set of information about industries that may be obtained from the Bureau of the Census is illustrated in Case 3.2. This is input-output information, which summarizes the flow of goods and services between sectors of the economy. This information is particularly helpful for economic and business applications, such as forecasting demand, identifying markets, and analyzing the effects of economic policy. A comprehensive treatment of input-output analysis is beyond the scope of this book, but the interested reader may refer to a 1984 U.S. Government Printing Office publication titled, *Detailed Input-Output Structure of the U.S. Economy: 1977, Volumes I and II.*

INTERNATIONAL DATA SOURCES

Many national governments collect census data similar to those obtained in the United States. For most of the developed nations in the world, data are available and reasonably accurate. Unfortunately, relatively few countries other than industrialized nations have collected data comparable to those available in the United States. Data collection in many Third World countries either is not done or is of recent origin. Data collection, however, is improving substantially throughout the world. The countries themselves, as well as outside organizations (e.g., the United Nations), are interested in such information, and this has prompted the establishment of data collection on an international scale.

There are three critical limitations of data obtained in many countries. First, there are few data available. Until the United Nations began collecting world economic data, only rough estimates of such fundamental statistics as population and income were available. Even in some developed nations, detailed information on industry, energy consumption, and housing may not be available or may be of very recent origin.

Another problem with secondary data in other nations is a lack of reliability. Official statistics can sometimes reflect national pride and international political considerations rather than reality. Tax and trade policies within a country may provide an incentive to distort figures reported to government counters. For example, when taxes are levied on production, it is to the advantage of a firm to underreport production. The Organization for Economic Cooperation and Development (OECD) is among the older sources of international economic data, and its data are among the most accurate. Yet it is criticized frequently for developing and presenting information that is consistent with the official policies and positions on issues of its members.

In the United States, reasonably reliable and valid data are readily available and are collected on a routine and (for the most part) timely basis. Reasonably reliable data are also available for much of western Europe, Canada, Australia, New Zealand, and Japan. In other nations, data may be collected infrequently and on idiosyncratic schedules. Another problem is that the rapid changes being experienced by many countries may quickly invalidate data. In addition, erratic scheduling of collection procedures may make it difficult to identify and to follow trends. Historical data may not be defined in the same manner from occasion to occasion.

Noncomparability of data is a serious problem when one is making comparisons across information from multiple sources. National governments often differ in both the methods employed to collect data and the definition of categories. Surveys are practical data-gathering tools in literate societies, but not in others. Thus data that might be obtained directly from an individual in a literate society may have to be collected by some other means in a nonliterate society, a difference that creates some noncomparability. On most occasions, such differences do not create problems, but one should not be surprised to find them.

When seeking data on the socioeconomic characteristics of nations, a good place to start is with the information provided by the United Nations. Table 3.4 summarizes some of the reports available through the United Nations and its affiliated agencies. A complete listing of UN publications may be found in the *Directory of United Nations Information Systems and Services* (1991). Another helpful document is the *Directory of International Statistics* (1982), which provides an overview of the statistical activities of the UN, including a listing of the statistical series compiled by the UN and a discussion of methodological standards.

The OECD produces numerous statistical reports and data tapes relevant to the socioeconomic characteristics of its members, as do numerous other international cooperatives. An excellent guide to much of this literature may be found in *Statistics Sources,* described in Table 3.1.

SUMMARY

This chapter provided a review of census data made available by the U.S. government and focused on the Bureau of the Census, along with ways of accessing census data. In addition, two major innovations for the 1990 decennial population census were discussed—availability of information on CD-ROM and the introduction of the TIGER digital map

Table 3.4
Selected Sources of International Demographic and Economic Data Available From the United Nations and Other Sources

Demographic Yearbook

Published annually by the United Nations, this text is a primary source of demographic data regarding 218 countries. The data describe population changes such as rate of increase, birthrates and death rates, migration, and marriages and divorces. Tables are presented that contain information on international migration statistics.

Disability Statistics Compendium

This UN publication presents detailed national data on disability from more than 50 countries or areas covering 12 major demographic and socioeconomic topics, including age, sex, residence, marital status, educational attainment, economic activity, type of living arrangements, household characteristics, causes of impairment, and special aids used by disabled persons. An overview of national practices, summary tables, and graphics are also provided.

Index to International Public Opinion 1988-89

Published annually by Survey Research Consulting International, Inc., and Greenwood Press, this publication contains data collected in more than 100 countries. This information is obtained by the firm's own surveys as well as by other surveys that may have been done. Respondents are categorized by such factors as age, sex, education, and income.

Industrial Statistics Yearbook

Published in two volumes. Volume 1 presents an annual compilation on world industry that includes information on major items of industrial activity and structure for more than 100 countries, classified by branch of activity. Also included are international tables on index numbers of industrial production and employment. Volume 2 presents internationally comparable information on the production of more than 550 industrial commodities for approximately 200 countries or areas. Both volumes are published by the United Nations.

United Nations Statistical Yearbook

Published annually by the United Nations since 1949, this publication provides statistics about the world regarding population, human resources, agriculture, forestry, fishing, industrial production, mining and quarrying, manufacturing, construction, energy, internal and external trade, transportation, communication, consumption, wages and prices, balance of payments, finance, housing, health, education, and science. *World Statistics in Brief,* available since 1976, is an annual summary of some of the most frequently used data in the yearbook.

World Economic Survey

This annual publication is a comprehensive review and analysis of world economic conditions and trends. Separate data are presented for developing countries, centrally planned economies, and developed market economies. Published by the United Nations.

(Continued)

Table 3.4 Continued

World Health Statistics Annual

Published by the World Health Organization and the Statistical Office of the United Nations, this publication provides information on vital statistics, causes of death, infectious diseases, health personnel, and hospital statistics.

International Trade Yearbook

Provides basic information for individual countries' external trade performance in terms of overall trends in current value as well as in volume and price, the importance of trading partners, and the significance of individual commodities imported or exported. Also published are basic summary tables showing, inter alia, the contribution of trade of each country to the trade of its region and of the world, analyzing the flow of trade between countries, and describing the fluctuations of the prices at which goods are moved internationally. The volume contains trade information on more than 150 countries. Published by the United Nations.

Monthly Bulletin of Statistics

A monthly publication of the United Nations reporting on population, human resources, transportation, trade, income, and finance. Provides current economic and social data for many of the tables published in the *United Nations Statistical Yearbook*. Quarterly data for significant world and regional aggregates are included regularly.

---

base system. An important section discussed methods of how to estimate population while one is waiting for the next census to be published. Also included was a review of the Standard Industrial Classification System (SIC) codes and of the availability of international data sources.

CASE 3.1

Using Census Data for Small Areas: The Location of a Playground[1]

Situation

A city parks and recreation director was recently appointed in a metropolitan area of about 100,000 people. The central city, Middletown, has about 65,000 inhabitants. The immediate task of the park director is to present a plan to the city manager for locating a new city playground in a neighborhood with a large number of children from low-income families where there are insufficient play areas. The playgrounds would be used regularly by 5- to 14-year-olds. The plan must be presented to the city council with documentation for the recommendation.

What Does the Park Director Need to Know?

- Where do the playground users live in the city?
- Where are the existing playgrounds?
- Where is land available for a new playground?
- Where are the neighborhoods with large numbers of children from low-income families?

Where Should the Park Director Go to Get Her Information?

Some information is available from her own office. For instance, the location of existing playgrounds is known. Therefore, on a large map of the city, she draws in the boundaries of the existing parks. To determine where land is available, the park director goes to the city planning office and discusses the problem with the director, who shows her a map of all existing vacant land sites. The two identify several possible locations, which they then map onto a cellophane sheet to overlay on the map of existing park locations (see Figure 3.2).

The park director still needs to know where in the city low-income families with children live. One option is to purchase this information from a company that maintains a geodemographic data base, such as Claritas Corporation's PRIZM service. Another less expensive possibility is a hands-on approach suggested by the city planner, which is to consult the census data. The census reports average ages and incomes of city residents living in neighborhoodlike areas called "census tracts." The planner explains that this information can be found in the census tract report. In the top left corner of the report is the code "PHC(1)," which references this series of census reports. The *P* and *H* together in the code indicate that the report includes data from both the population and housing censuses.

They open the PHC(1) report and look at the table that gives age data for both males and females (referred to as "age by sex") for the entire county, the city, the remainder of the county ("balance"), and the individual census tracts. Studying the table further, they see that two lines are labeled "Male, 5 to 9 years" and "Male, 10 to 14 years," with equivalent lines for females. The park director simply needs to add the columns on the office calculator to obtain the total number of children aged 5 to 14 living in these areas.

They then turn to the back of the report, where there is a map showing the boundaries of the census tracts and the tract numbers referred to in the census tables. Next, from the table of contents, they identify a table titled "Income Characteristics of the Population: 1980." This table shows

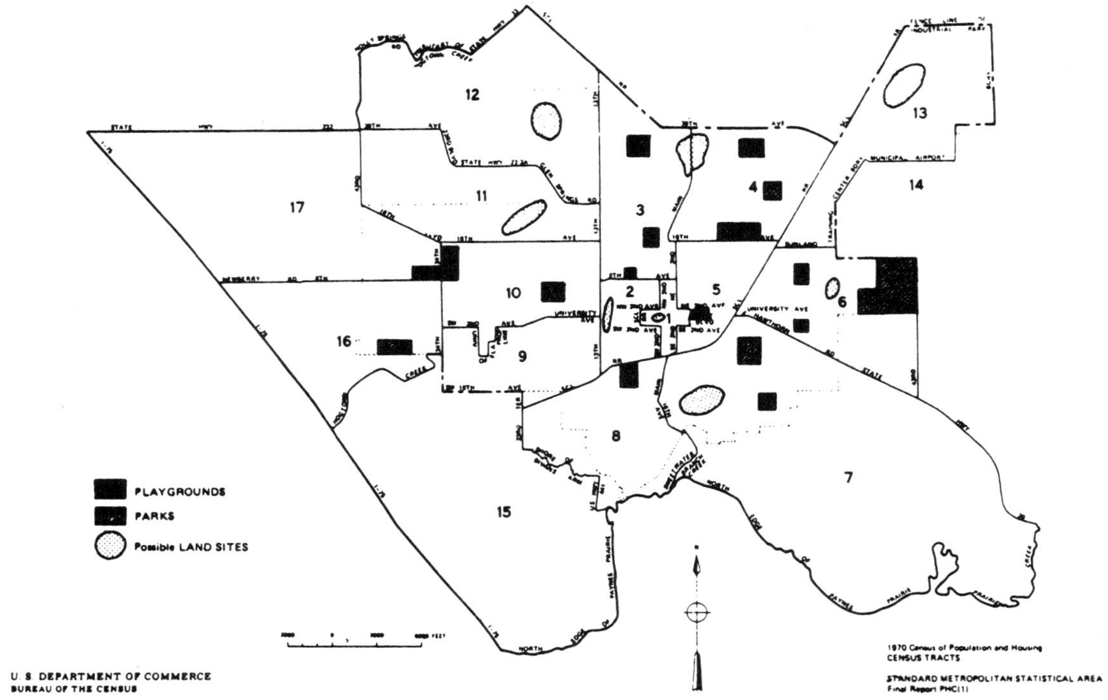

Figure 3.2. Existing Playgrounds, Parks, and Possible Land Sites, 1971: Census Tracts in Middletown and Vicinity

52

the income distribution and other data on individuals earning "income below the poverty level." The poverty index provides a range of low-income cutoffs with adjustments for family size, sex of the family head, number of children under age 18, and farm versus nonfarm residency.

The income characteristic of each tract can be described in any of the following ways: (a) an income distribution, (b) the mean or median income, (c) the number of families whose incomes are from public assistance or public welfare, (d) the percentage of families with a ratio of family income to the poverty level of less than 1.0, (e) the number of families with incomes below the poverty level, and (f) the number of families with income below the poverty level and with children under the age of 18.

The park director studies each possibility in light of her particular needs. She must first decide on the definition of "low-income families." She can use the 1980 census poverty index or her own operational definition, using the income data in options (a) through (f) above. If she selects from options (a) through (e), however, she can only find areas with a high concentration of low-income families. She will not know whether children are present (a recommendation to place a playground in a predominantly low-income elderly neighborhood would not win the park director a promotion!). Therefore she must choose option (f), which is a count of families with children under 18 whose family incomes are below the poverty level. She cannot directly determine the number of 5- to 14-year-olds from this summary. Thus she has the following two choices:

1. Use the counts of low-income families with children under 18 combined with counts of children aged 5 to 14. Then make an approximation of the number of 5- to 14-year-olds in low-income families. Such an approximation can be made by multiplying the mean number of such children by the number of low-income families with children. Then, using the age data for the total population, compute the proportion of the under-18 population that is 5 to 14 years old and, finally, the proportion of these children living in low-income families. The appendix to this case study illustrates this method of approximation. Note that the mean number of children in a family varies considerably, and that, therefore, a decision based solely on the number of families might be misleading.

2. Get the data in the exact form desired by requesting a "special tabulation" from the Census Bureau. The park director called the Census Bureau for a rough estimate and found that a special tabulation would cost about $3,000. She decided that in this particular case it was not worth the expense. With the aid of a simple calculator, she filled in the compu-

tation sheet shown in Table 3.5 to estimate the number of children aged 5 to 14 in low-income families. As she developed the computation sheet, she noticed that tracts 6, 7, 8, 11, 12, 14, 16, and 17 had data listed in three places: "Middletown," the "balance of the county," and "totals for split tracts." That is, these split tracts crossed the city boundaries, and thus separate data were given for the part of the tract in the city of Middletown, for the part outside the city, and for the entire tract, respectively. For this study, she used only the data for the Middletown sections of the tracts.

The city planner discussed some aspects of the data of which the user should be aware. The census was taken in April of 1980. After several years, the characteristics of populations change, especially in small geographic areas, as people age and move in and out of the area. Lacking a source of more recent data, the park director could only assume that the relationships among the tracts were relatively the same as they were in 1980.

Census data can never be viewed as exact. In any mass statistical operation such as the decennial census, human and mechanical errors occur, although efforts are made to keep these nonsampling errors at an acceptably low level. Also, some data are based on a sample and thus are subject to sampling errors as well. Sometimes data are omitted and replaced by ellipses in the data tables. This occurs (a) when the number of people in a certain category is so small that it might be possible to identify them if the information were released, and thus the data are withheld to maintain confidentiality; or (b) when the base of a derived figure (e.g., the median or percentage) is too small to provide reliable data, and therefore the statistics are not computed to maintain data quality.

It is also important to recognize that the computations carried out are based on the following assumptions:

1. The census gives us information based on the poverty level. The computations assume that "low income" and the "poverty level" are the same thing. It could be argued, however, that this understates the number of low-income people, because people above the poverty level can still earn very low incomes. The question then is whether these low-income people who are above the poverty level are living in different areas than those below the poverty level. The results could change if this is so.

2. The computations also assume that the proportion of 5- to 14-year-old children in the population of children under 18 (i.e., in column 4 of Table 3.5) is the same for poverty-level families as families at other income levels. If this is not so, the results again might be misleading.

Table 3.5

Computation of an Approximation of the Number of Children Aged 5 to 14 in Low-Income Families in Middletown, 1980

Tract Number	(1) Children Under 18 in Low-Income Families[a]	(2) Total Number of 5-14 Year Olds	(3) Total Number 18 Year Olds	(4) Population Under Under 18, Aged 5-14	(5) Estimated Number of Children Aged 5-14 in Low-Income Families
Total MSA	7,137[b]	18,861	32,923	0.57	4,068
Middletown	3,699	10,098	17,922	0.56	2,071
0001	—	67[c]	123	0.54	—
0002	(2.65)(221) = 586	621	1,140	0.54	316
0003	(2.49)(70) = 174	797	1,486	0.54	94
0004	(2.17)(35) = 76	1,360	2,286	0.59	45
0005	(2.12)(77) = 163	705	1,267	0.56	91
0006	(3.46)(231) = 799	1,053	1,779	0.59	471
0007	(3.21)(391) = 1,255	1,602	2,726	0.59	740
0008	(1.82)(33) = 60	174	395	0.44	26
0009	(1.60)(159) = 254	231	820	0.28	71
0010	(1.85)(39) = 72	793	1,370	0.58	42
0011	—	478	810	0.59	—
0012	(2.76)(51) = 141	397	762	0.52	73
0013	—	550	820	0.67	—
0014	—	4	6	0.66	—
0016	(2.00)(43) = 86	708	1,169	0.61	52
0017	—	558	963	0.58	—

a. These do not total 3,699 because of suppression in tracts 0001 and 0017.

b. Middletown plus the balance do not add to 7,137 because of rounding.

c. As an example of this calculation: 67 = 17 + 13 + 8 + 29, which is a summation of males and females aged 5-9 and 10-14.

3. A fundamental question is which age group will use the playground the most. These computations assume that children between the ages of 5 and 14 all use playgrounds with equal frequency.

4. Finally, the data refer to one point in time. Therefore, planners using the data can only assume that they reflect future population characteristics.

The results of the computations in Table 3.5 indicate that only three tracts are serious prospects for the playground (assuming validity of the numbers). These are as follows:

	Estimated Number of Children Aged 5 to 14
Tract Number	in Low-Income Families
0007	740
0006	471
0002	316

These results must then be compared with the current playground, parks, and the possible land sites given in Figure 3.2. This examination indicates the following:

1. Tract 7 has a land site, but already has one playground and one park.

2. Tract 6 has a land site, but already has two playgrounds.

3. Tract 2 has a land site and no parks or playground. There is a playground in tract 5 not far from tract 2; however, it is across many busy streets from tract 2 and thus is not very accessible.

Tract 7 appears to be the best selection because it contains neither a playground nor a park.

Appendix: Computational Illustration

Data are not always published in the exact form desired, but it is often possible to compute what is needed. In this case study, for example, the park director wanted an approximation of the number of 5- to 14-year-olds in low-income families. The description below illustrates a method for doing this if you are willing to assume that the proportion of children aged 5 to 14 is the same in the total population as it is in the low-income-family population. (The steps below relate to the columns in Table 3.5.)

1. Compute the number of related children under 18 in the low-income families:

   Column 1 = (mean number of related children under 18 years)(number of families with income below the poverty level with related children under 18 years).

   For the MSA, this is: (2.88)(2,478) = 7,137

2. Compute the total population aged 5 to 14 years:

   Column 2 = (males 5 to 9 years) + (males 10 to 14 years) + (females 5 to 9 years) + (females 10 to 14 years)

   For this MSA, this is: 4,809 + 4,791 + 4,588 + 4,673 = 18,861

3. The number of persons under 18 years is shown under the heading in Column 3.

   For this MSA, the number of persons under 18 years is 32,923.

4. Compute the proportion of the total under-18 population that is aged 5 to 14 years:

   Column 4 = $\dfrac{\text{column 2}}{\text{column 3}}$

   For the MSA, this is: $\dfrac{18,861}{32,923} = .57$

5. Compute an estimate of the number of 5- to 14-year-olds in low-income families:

   Column 5 = (Column 4)(Column 1)

   For this MSA, this is: (.57)(7,137) = 4,068

CASE 3.2

Unlimited Data Research Company[2]

Objective

To predict the potential market in 1991 to sell paper and allied products to merchant wholesalers and in retail trade.

Kind of Business

A research company engaged in economic studies, industrial development, and marketing research.

Problem

The research company was engaged by a paper manufacturer to estimate the market potential for paper and allied products to merchant wholesalers and in retail trade. First, because the manufacturer had sales representatives and needed to determine its sales force, it wanted to know the quantity of paper and allied products consumed directly by various trades. Second, in early 1991, the research company was asked to project total 1991 requirements, both direct and indirect, of wholesale and retail trade. Finally, the research organization was requested to project the manufacturer's share of the market given the fact that, based on past history, the manufacturer normally accounts for 15% of the total market for paper and allied products.

Sources of Data

1. "Input-Output Structure of the U.S. Economy 1977," *Survey of Current Business* (May 1984)
2. *1991 U.S. Industrial Outlook* (with projections to 1991)
3. *Monthly Wholesale Trade: Sales and Inventories* (March 1991).

Assumptions.

1. The relative demand for paper and allied products by the retail trades is estimated effectively by the *1991 U.S. Industrial Outlook* publication.
2. That the actual estimate of merchant wholesaler sales for January-April 1991 obtained from *Monthly Wholesale Trade: Sales and Inventories* can be multiplied by 3 to gain a reasonable estimate of merchant wholesaler sales for the entire year of 1991.
3. To compute both direct and indirect use of paper and allied products by wholesale and retail trade, the research company used gross profit (or gross margin), which is estimated to be almost 25% of sales. To demonstrate the links between producing and consuming industries and the effect on final markets in the input-output tables, commodities are shown as if moving directly from producer to user, bypassing trade. Therefore, the output of trade is measured in terms of total margins (i.e., operating expenses plus profits).

Procedure

According to the March report of *Monthly Wholesale Trade: Sales and Inventories* (source 3), merchant wholesaler sales in 1991 will be $1,721 billion. Retail sales are estimated to be about $1,982 billion, as projected by the 1991 edition of *U.S. Industrial Outlook* (source 2). The combined total in 1991 will therefore be $3,703 billion. Because the manufacturer wanted to know the amount of paper and products consumed directly by wholesale and retail trade, the research company first computed 25% (gross profit) of $3,703 billion, which came to approximately $926 billion. Then, from Table 3.6 (which was reproduced from table 3 of the input-output study in source 1), it was found that for each dollar of gross profit of wholesale and retail trade, $0.0058 worth of paper was consumed directly. Therefore the total amount consumed directly by the wholesale and retail trades was $5.37 billion ($926 billion × 0.0058). This represents only the cost of paper products that are used directly by the two trades and does not include products used indirectly by the manufacturers of food and kindred products or by nonfood merchandise that is distributed via the wholesale and retail trades method.

In addition, the research company computed estimates of total requirements of paper and allied products, including those used by processors of other materials consumed by manufacturers. This was measured by using the direct and indirect costs shown in Table 3.7 (reproduced from table 5 of the input-output study) and was found to be $0.01342. Thus total requirements in 1991 were estimated to be $12.43 billion ($926 billion × 0.01342). The paper manufacturer reported that its share of the total market for paper and allied products to the wholesale and retail trades was 15%. The research company therefore projected the manufacturer's share of the total market to be $1.864 billion ($12.43 billion × 0.15).

Conclusion

Based upon projected demand for paper and allied products by the trades, the manufacturer drafted a proposed plan for enlarging the plant, adding more salespersons, redefining sales territories, and expanding other facets of business operations.

EXERCISES

Exercise 3.1: Go to your local library and access TIGER, either on-line or on CD-ROM, and use the system for an application relevant to your business or interests.

Exercise 3.2: What sources of information provided by the U.S. Bureau of the Census would you consult for data on the energy consumption patterns of households and organizations in a particular country?

Table 3.6
Direct Requirements per Dollar of Gross Output, 1977

Commodity number	For the composition of inputs to an industry, read the column for that industry	Transportation and warehousing	Communications, except radio and TV	Radio and TV broadcasting	Electric, gas, water, and sanitary services	Wholesale and retail trade	Finance and insurance
	Industry number	65	66	67	68	69	70
1	Livestock and livestock products	0.00001					
2	Other agricultural products	.00003				.00005	
3	Forestry and fishery products	(*)				.00001	
4	Agricultural, forestry, and fishery services	.00003	.00001	.00004	.00007	.00159	.00002
5	Iron and ferroalloy ores mining						
6	Nonferrous metal ores mining				.05743		
7	Coal mining	.00003			.12451		
8	Crude petroleum and natural gas	.00063					
9	Stone and clay mining and quarrying						
10	Chemical and fertilizer mineral mining						
11	New construction						
12	Maintenance and repair construction	.03662	.03645	.00352	.03515	.00666	.00271
13	Ordnance and accessories	.00001	(*)		(*)	.00001	.00001
14	Food and kindred products	.00058		.00041	.00005	.00085	.00005
15	Tobacco manufactures						
16	Broad and narrow fabrics, yarn and thread mills	.00002				(*)	
17	Miscellaneous textile goods and floor coverings	.00049				.00015	
18	Apparel	.00073	.00069	.00001	.00004	.00020	
19	Miscellaneous fabricated textile products	.00058				.00008	.00062
20	Lumber and wood products, except containers	.00014			.00056	.00108	
21	Wood containers	(*)				.00005	
22	Household furniture						
23	Other furniture and fixtures						
24	Paper and allied products, except containers	.00060	.00066	.00051	.00041	.00580	.00299
25	Paperboard containers and boxes	.00029	.00017	.00004	.00004	.00179	.00001
26	Printing and publishing	.00209	.00265	.00168	.00061	.00403	.01271
27	Chemicals and selected chemical products	.00092	.00014	.00086	.00303	.00007	.00004
28	Plastics and synthetic materials						
29	Drugs, cleaning and toilet preparations	.00003	.00071		.00001	.00035	.00004
30	Paints and allied products	.00018	.00054				
31	Petroleum refining and related industries	.06969	.00224	.00076	.07670	.01315	.00333
32	Rubber and miscellaneous plastics products	.00767	.00126	.00007	.00057	.00275	.00041
33	Leather tanning and finishing						
34	Footwear and other leather products	.00003	.00001	.00005	.00001	.00023	.00006
35	Glass and glass products	.00016	.00004	.00001	.00001	.00027	.00006
36	Stone and clay products	.00042	.00022		.00007	.00017	.00001
37	Primary iron and steel manufacturing	.00230	.00001			.00002	.00001
38	Primary nonferrous metals manufacturing	.00076	.00118		.00018		
39	Metal containers				.00004	.00030	
40	Heating, plumbing, and structural metal products					.00005	

*Less than 0.000005
SOURCE: *Survey of Current Business* (May 1984)

Table 3.7
Total Requirements (Direct and Indirect) per Dollar of Delivery to Final Demand, 1977

Industry number	Each entry represents the output required, directly and indirectly, from the industry named at the beginning of the row for each dollar of delivery to final demand of the commodity named at the head of the column.	Transportation and warehousing	Communications, except radio and TV	Radio and TV broadcasting	Electric, gas, water, and sanitary services	Wholesale and retail trade	Finance and insurance
	Commodity number	65	66	67	68	69	70
1	Livestock and livestock products	0.00187	0.00070	0.00488	0.00096	0.00284	0.00179
2	Other agricultural products	.00181	.00066	.01074	.00099	.00243	.00147
3	Forestry and fishery products	.00056	.00030	.00052	.00060	.00060	.00035
4	Agricultural, forestry, and fishery services	.00075	.00045	.00163	.00095	.00204	.00045
5	Iron and ferroalloy ores mining	.00081	.00031	.00023	.00082	.00023	.00014
6	Nonferrous metal ores mining	.00079	.00053	.00045	.00081	.00027	.00020
7	Coal mining	.00318	.00158	.00213	.08756	.00270	.00179
8	Crude petroleum and natural gas	.06723	.00780	.01098	.23650	.01973	.01022
9	Stone and clay mining and quarrying	.00147	.00083	.00055	.00190	.00051	.00032
10	Chemical and fertilizer mineral mining	.00044	.00016	.00029	.00062	.00020	.00015
11	New construction						
12	Maintenance and repair construction	.05814	.04212	.02148	.08114	.01778	.01150
13	Ordnance and accessories	.00023	.00029	.00010	.00010	.00009	.00008
14	Food and kindred products	.00647	.00235	.01326	.00318	.00962	.00635
15	Tobacco manufactures	(*)	(*)	(*)	(*)	(*)	(*)
16	Broad and narrow fabrics, yarn and thread mills	.00234	.00101	.00186	.00118	.00120	.00134
17	Miscellaneous textile goods and floor coverings	.00154	.00042	.00065	.00069	.00063	.00043
18	Apparel	.00135	.00103	.00131	.00044	.00051	.00027
19	Miscellaneous fabricated textile products	.00096	.00020	.00053	.00023	.00033	.00092
20	Lumber and wood products, except containers	.00469	.00269	.00293	.00599	.00415	.00211
21	Wood containers	.00005	.00003	.00005	.00004	.00008	.00002
22	Household furniture	.00013	.00034	.00015	.00008	.00005	.00005
23	Other furniture and fixtures	.00016	.00008	.00007	.00013	.00005	.00004
24	Paper and allied products, except containers	.00635	.00419	.00615	.00478	.01342	.01228
25	Paperboard containers and boxes	.00196	.00096	.00134	.00139	.00308	.00101
26	Printing and publishing	.01129	.00854	.01265	.00650	.01808	.03138
27	Chemicals and selected chemical products	.01267	.00433	.00856	.01733	.00574	.00428
28	Plastics and synthetic materials	.00386	.00173	.00204	.00235	.00191	.00134
29	Drugs, cleaning and toilet preparations	.00118	.00110	.00082	.00131	.00102	.00070
30	Paints and allied products	.00177	.00146	.00061	.00176	.00064	.00041
31	Petroleum refining and related industries	.09266	.00824	.01105	.10706	.02264	.01076
32	Rubber and miscellaneous plastics products	.01312	.00485	.00472	.00585	.00555	.00291
33	Leather tanning and finishing	.00004	.00002	.00006	.00002	.00007	.00005
34	Footwear and other leather products	.00009	.00004	.00022	.00006	.00028	.00013
35	Glass and glass products	.00105	.00063	.00109	.00066	.00083	.00045
36	Stone and clay products	.00513	.00309	.00204	.00631	.00186	.00109
37	Primary iron and steel manufacturing	.01560	.00597	.00431	.01540	.00445	.00263
38	Primary nonferrous metals manufacturing	.00915	.00720	.00537	.00819	.00302	.00218
39	Metal containers	.00088	.00031	.00066	.00089	.00090	.00045
40	Heating, plumbing, and structural metal products	.00436	.00285	.00157	.00553	.00133	.00084

*Less than 0.000005
SOURCE: *Survey of Current Business* (May 1984)

Exercise 3.3: Find the most recent report of the *Census of Manufacturers* (1987). For your county, identify the number of firms that are engaged in the manufacture of household furniture (SIC 251), power equipment (SIC 34433 and 35111), and industrial organic chemicals (SIC 2865). How many banking firms (SIC 602) are there in your county? What industry is the largest in your county in terms of number of employees? In terms of sales?

Exercise 3.4: Your local city government is considering opening a group of day-care centers for elderly citizens. Using only secondary data, assess the demand for such centers and identify potential sites for locating them.

Exercise 3.5: Identify the demographic characteristics of the leisure travelers in the United States who do most of the traveling.

Exercise 3.6: What nations of the world are in the greatest need of assistance with increasing crop production per acre?

NOTES

1. This case is an adaptation of a case prepared by Cynthia Murray Taeuber of the U.S. Bureau of the Census.

2. This case is an adaptation of a case originally presented in the U.S. Bureau of the Census, Department of Commerce, Industry and Trade Administration publication titled *Measuring Markets: A Guide to the Use of Federal and State Statistical Data* (1979).

4

Government Information, Part II: Other Government Documents

A wide range of data, information, and statistics is provided by government agencies other than the Census Bureau. Federal, state, and local government agencies, the judicial system, and legislative bodies produce vast quantities of highly reliable information. International agencies such as the United Nations provide information about nations other than the United States and about global issues. This chapter discusses these sources of data and means for identifying and accessing this information.

The Bureau of the Census is only one of the many federal agencies that generate reports, data, and other types of information. Indeed, despite the volume of census data, it represents only a fraction of the information issued by federal government agencies. The Freedom of Information Act of 1966 opens numerous sources of data to public scrutiny that otherwise would be unavailable. Under the act, administrative agencies in the executive branch of the federal government must release any identifiable records unless the information falls within one of nine exemption categories. A discussion of the procedure for obtaining information under the Freedom of Information Act is provided later in this chapter.

Not all information generated by governmental bodies is collected and reported as carefully as the census data. Government agencies are frequently prone to find answers to questions, no matter how unrealistic, rather than to admit not knowing. A widely quoted figure on the cost of air pollution was apparently based on a single study in Pittsburgh early in the century (Wasson, 1974). This figure was extrapolated to a national level and submitted in a report to Congress. Generally, the most reliable government information is that generated by regularly scheduled surveys and studies. A number of agencies publish regular statistical reports, including those listed below.

AGENCIES THAT PUBLISH STATISTICAL REPORTS

The Federal Reserve System

The Federal Reserve System issues a monthly publication, the *Federal Reserve Bulletin,* which was first published in May 1915. The publication contains announcements and articles regarding the actions of the Federal Reserve Board of Governors and also provides the minutes of meetings of the Federal Open Market Committee. The publication reports statistics in various financial arenas, including the consumer sector, business, government, and real estate. Specifics include data on policy instruments (including interest rates), federal reserve banks, monetary and credit aggregates, commercial banking institutions, financial markets, federal finance, securities markets and corporate finance, consumer installment credit, flow of funds, international statistics, and international interest and exchange rates. The publication is available on-line through ABI/INFORM and Management Contents. The *Federal Reserve Chart Book,* issued quarterly since 1976, and the *Federal Reserve Historical Chart Book,* issued annually, also provide a variety of data on financial statistics and consumer buying

Department of Agriculture

The Department of Agriculture (DOA) publishes three major volumes each year: *Agricultural Statistics, Crop Production,* and *Agricultural Prices.* These three publications provide information on the number and type of farm operations, the quantity of production of various crops and livestock, and the real and expected values of particular crops, respectively. The DOA also publishes monthly reports and numerous special studies. For example, *Foreign Agricultural Trade of the United States,* published bimonthly, provides data on the value and quantity of imported and exported agricultural commodities. These reports are used widely by economists, rural sociologists, and government and business planners. The *World Agriculture Situation and Outlook Report* analyzes the state of the world agriculture industry through the use of text and empirical statistics. Specifically, developments and trends within specific countries, regions, and specific commodities are reviewed. The DOA also publishes *Agricultural Outlook, Economic Indicators of the Farm Sector, Foreign Agriculture, World Agricultural Supply and Demand Estimates,* and the *Yearbook of Agriculture.* All of these publications are indexed in the American Statistics Index (ASI).

Department of Labor

The Labor Department conducts detailed studies of family expenditure patterns in order to update the Consumer Price Index. These studies are carried out regularly, and the results are published. The *Monthly Labor Review,* published since 1915, contains statistics on employment and unemployment; labor turnover; wages and hours worked; occupational injury and illness data; work stoppages; retail, wholesale, and commodity price indexes; and other current labor statistics. *The Directory of Occupational Titles*, published sporadically since 1939, contains reports of job analyses of more than 20,000 occupations. This document includes information about activities and trade requirements of relatively standardized jobs. The Bureau of Labor Statistics within the department makes projections, by occupation, of labor market conditions and future occupation supply. These data are used widely for human resources planning and for developing and implementing employment policies.

Employment and Earnings Statistics for States and Areas is an annual publication of more than 7,500 statistical series on payroll employment by industry. It also reports 3,300 series on hours and earnings of production workers by industry. All available data for the given time period are reported. Information is categorized by state and by 202 major areas. A companion volume, *Employment and Earnings Statistics for the United States,* is an annual summary at the national level; two monthly publications, *Employment and Earnings* and *Monthly Report on the Labor Force*, provide updates. The *Handbook of Labor Statistics* is a compilation of the Bureau of Labor Statistics major data series. Data sections specifically focus upon employment, unemployment, employee characteristics, employees on nonagricultural payrolls, productivity, compensation, and selective statistics on foreign labor. The *Occupational Outlook Handbook,* published on a biennial basis by the Department of Labor, provides information regarding prospective employment in terms of job expectations and conditions for approximately 200 occupations. The *Area Wage Survey,* published annually, provides a survey of occupational earnings and supplementary benefits for plant and office occupations in six broad classifications (manufacturing, public utilities, wholesale trade, retail trade, finance, and service industries). More than 90 MSAs and PMSAs are covered. Finally, *Unemployment in States and Local Areas* gives monthly estimates of unemployment for labor market areas, counties, and cities of 25,000 or more.

Department of Commerce

In addition to the substantial output of the Bureau of the Census, the Department of Commerce produces numerous studies and reports. It has published the *Survey of Current Business* on a monthly basis since 1921. This document provides a comprehensive statistical summary of national income and product accounts in the United States. It specifically contains more than 2,600 statistical series covering such information as commodity prices, construction and real estate, general business indicators, domestic trade, employment, population, finance, transportation, communications, and international transactions. *Highlights of U.S. Export and Import Trade*, published on a monthly basis by the Department of Commerce, gives the reader in-depth statistical reports of U.S. exports and imports having values of about $1,000. The data are grouped by month, year, type of product (on both a specific and general basis) as well as geographical locations (on both a regional and country basis). This publication serves as a comprehensive reference guide to both import and export statistics.

Another specialized publication of the Department of Commerce is the *County and City Data Book,* now available on CD-ROM. Published on an irregular basis, it provides a convenient source of statistics on a city and county basis, including population, income education, employment, and housing. *Business Statistics* is published every 2 years and provides a historical record of the data series reported in the monthly *Survey of Current Business. County Business Patterns* is a joint publication of the Department of Commerce and the Department of Health and Human Services. It contains statistics on the number and types of businesses by county; it also provides information on employment and payroll. Finally, the *Country Market Survey* (CMS) provides a series of reports regarding classes of products in specific countries. The CMS provides the reader with information regarding an assessment of the market for the product in terms of competition, end users, and market practices, as well as an overview of the economy of the country. It also includes a list of agencies and organizations to be contacted for additional information. This publication is particularly useful for those marketers who have entered or are considering entering foreign markets, thereby taking a multinational perspective to their business.

A special division of the Department of Commerce, the National Technical Information Service (NTIS), collects and disseminates technical report information generated by government-funded research. NTIS maintains a data bank of more than 250,000 abstracts of federally

sponsored technical reports published since 1964. Customized bibliographic services are available. NTIS also distributes a bibliography of
translations on significant research literature published in other languages. NTIS publishes the *National Environmental Statistical Report*,
which summarizes environmental data and trends. Finally, *Ethnic Statistics: A Compendium of Reference Sources* abstracts 92 federal statistical data resources that contain ethnic or racial data. A users' guide, *Ethnic
Statistics: Using National Data Resources for Ethnic Studies,* is also
available.

Department of Health and Human Services

The Department of Health and Human Services publishes the *Monthly
Vital Statistics Report* and an annual summary volume, *Vital Statistics
of the United States.* These publications provide information on births,
deaths, marriages, divorces, and a variety of statistics related to health
on a state-by-state basis.

Council of Economic Advisors

Economic Indicators, a monthly publication of this agency, includes
charts and tables with general economic data related to personal consumption expenditures, gross national product, national income, interest rates, federal finance, international statistics, and other categories.
This publication has two supplements, *Supplement to Economic Indicators* and *Descriptive Supplement to Economic Indicators.* The council
also compiles an annual report that reviews economic policy and provides forecasts. This annual report is part of the *Economic Report of the
President.*

Internal Revenue Service

Statistics of Income: Corporation Income Tax Returns has been published annually by the Internal Revenue Service since 1916. This publication provides a detailed report on both foreign and domestic corporate income. Data are presented by industry and are classified by size
of total assets and size of business receipts, using an industry code similar
to the two- or three-digit SIC code. The IRS actually publishes several
different publications under the title of *Statistics of Income,* each relevant to a different type of tax return: individual, corporate, partnership,

or proprietorship. Finally, in terms of data on individual tax returns, the IRS now publishes an annual sourcebook that presents data on personal returns classified by demographic variables such as age, filing status, and type of form filed.

Bureau of Economic Analysis

The Bureau of Economic Analysis (BEA) publishes a monthly analysis of economic indicators entitled *Business Conditions Digest*. Each issue has three parts: (a) cyclical indicators, including indicators for various economic processes, composite indices of economic activity, and indices of diffusion and rates of change; (b) other important economic measures, including data on the labor force, employment and unemployment, government involvement in business activities, prices, wages, productivity, national income, and international transactions; and (c) appendices of historical data and special measures and factors. The bureau's *Handbook of Cyclical Indicators,* which is published on an irregular basis, collects information on about 300 time series that were published originally in *Business Conditions Digest.* This publication contains four parts that respectively deal with series descriptions; composite indices of leading, coincident, and lagging indicators; historical data; and reference materials. The BEA also publishes *Local Area Personal Income,* which presents estimates of total and per capita personal income for counties and metropolitan areas in nine volumes. Presented in Volume 1 are summaries for the nation, regions, and states; Volumes 2 through 9 deal respectively with each of eight BEA regions (New England, Midwest, Great Lakes, Plains, Southeast, Southwest, Rocky Mountain, and Far West).

Federal Communications Commission

Statistics of Communication Common Carriers is an annual report of financial and operating data concerning all common carriers engaged in interstate or foreign communication service. Included in this publication is information dealing with the number of telephones in the United States, along with developments, revenues, overseas communication service, and employee information. This is an excellent source for finding information about specific utility companies. Quarterly data are available in the *Quarterly Operating Data of Telephone Carriers* and the *Quarterly Operating Data of Telegraph Carriers.*

Department of Energy

The Energy Information Administration (EIA) publishes a semiannual guide to the data contained in its publications. *EIA Data Index: An Abstract Journal* and a companion publication, *EIA Publications Directory: A Users Guide,* are good introductions to the vast quantity of data collected by the Department of Energy. These data include actual and projected energy resource reserves, consumption, production, prices, supply and demand, and other information about U.S. energy production and use. Other Department of Energy publications include *Natural Gas Monthly; Petroleum Marketing Monthly; Petroleum Supply Annual; U.S. Crude Oil, Natural Gas, and Natural Gas Liquid Reserves;* and the *Weekly Petroleum Status Report.*

Securities and Exchange Commission

The Securities and Exchange Commission (SEC) collects volumes of information on individual corporations in the United States. This source is a good place to begin researching any domestic company selling stocks to the public. Documents may be obtained by mail for a nominal cost, and many libraries carry selected SEC documents. Among the more useful SEC documents are the following forms and reports filed by companies: 10-K, 10-Q, and 8-K.

Form 10-K, which is filed annually, includes information on the type of business the company is in, number of employees, estimates of competitors, names of executive officers and directors, locations of properties owned, changes in competitive conditions and product lines, research and development expenditures, patents and trademarks, sales, revenues, profits, income, and total assets. Forms 10-Q and 8-K provide updates for Form 10-K between filings. All of these forms provide a wealth of information about individual companies. A reasonably comprehensive picture of an industry can often be constructed by examining the Form 10-K reports of the competing companies. These forms may be obtained by requesting the specific form, for a particular filing period, for the corporation(s) of interest. Such data are often quite useful to economists studying specific industries and to business planners interested in competitors.

National Science Board

Science Indicators presents data on public attitudes toward science and technology, science and engineering personnel, resources for basic research, industrial research and development, and international research.

Congressional Information Service

The *Statistical Reference Index* is a selective guide to statistics and data compiled by organizations other than the federal government. It is published monthly. *The American Statistics Index: A Comprehensive Guide and Index to the Statistical Publications of the U.S. Government* is a monthly guide to the statistical publications of the federal government.

State and Local Governments

The federal government is not the only governmental source of information. State and local government units also obtain substantial data on topics relevant to their concerns. States often publish statistical abstracts. In addition, the *Encyclopedia of Geographic Information Sources* (U.S. volume published in 1986; international volume published in 1988) is a useful guide to periodicals, directories, and statistics about states and cities. Finally, data regarding automobile registrations, business licenses, marriages, and the like generally are tabulated by states and local governments and are available in one form or another.

Courts

Records of the judiciary system are often open to the public, although this is not always the case. In federal and state courts, records are available from the court clerk's office. Each office maintains a judgment index that lists cases by plaintiff and defendant. The Supreme Court maintains a library, and there are regional depositories of court records throughout the country. Local court clerks' offices can usually assist in identifying the nearest regional depository.

INFORMATION ON GOVERNMENT GRANTS, CONTRACTS, AND ASSISTANCE

Frequently individuals are interested in learning about opportunities for supplying services to the government or obtaining assistance from government agencies. Academic researchers and institutions often want information on grants for research or training. Local and regional government bodies commonly wish to learn of federal assistance programs.

Business firms are interested in contract work, bids for equipment, and other commercial transactions of the federal government. A particularly useful guide to such information is the *United States Government Manual,* an official handbook of the federal government. The manual, published annually since 1935, contains descriptions of all federal agencies and their activities. The focus is on the legislative, executive, and judicial branches of the government; only limited information is given for independent, multinational, quasi-official, and other types of government organizations. A special section of the manual is called "Guide to Government Information" and explains how to keep in touch with U.S. government publications.

The sheer magnitude of federal programs has necessitated the publication of a guide to assistance programs. The *Catalog of Federal Domestic Assistance* (CFDA) is a comprehensive listing of federal programs and activities providing financial assistance or benefits to the public. Information on a wide range of programs is provided in the CFDA, ranging from grants and loans to insurance. Typical program information provided includes agency responsibility, objectives, eligibility requirements, and application and reward processes.

Persons or firms desiring to sell to the federal government should become familiar with the *Commerce Business Daily* (CBD). CBD, published by the Department of Commerce since 1954, is the means by which the federal government announces opportunities to bid on the procurement of equipment, materials, services, contract research, and the like. Department of Defense projects expected to cost at least $10,000, and other departmental or agency projects expected to cost at least $5,000, must be advertised in CBD. Announcements of contracts and awards also are published. The Office of Management and Budget publishes the *Catalog of Federal Domestic Assistance,* which also provides information on federal programs and federal financial assistance. The Office of Procurement and Technical Assistance publishes, on an irregular basis, the *U.S. Government Purchasing and Sales Directory.* This directory provides an overview of information for any small business that wants to sell products to the federal government.

The *Federal Register* is a daily publication of the federal government. It announces newly proposed programs, recently adopted regulations, and changes in existing programs and policies. The *Federal Register* is of particular importance to social science researchers because it makes grant announcements. Individual agencies often have their own publication vehicles as well. For example, the National Institute of Health publishes *NIH Research Contracting Process* and *Guide to Grant and*

Award Programs, and the National Endowment for the Arts publishes *Cultural Directory: Guide to Federal Funds and Services for Cultural Activities.*

A rather substantial industry has developed to monitor government programs. For fees ranging from modest to quite high, various members of this industry will provide information on specific government programs. Several firms now provide on-line computer search capabilities that allow one to identify information relevant to a particular agency program quickly (see Chapter 6). Recently, government products have also become available on CD-ROM (Chapter 6 also provides a detailed discussion of this new technology). As an example, the 1988 *City and County Data Book* is available in this medium, as is the 1987 economic census. The *National Trade Data Bank* on CD-ROM is particularly useful, because the software allows one to access data from the *U.S. Industrial Outlook* and other sources. Finally, the Census Bureau is planning to put a significant amount of data from the 1990 census on CD-ROM.

One particularly useful publication in terms of grants is the *Annual Register of Grant Support,* published by Marquis Who's Who. This publication is the only annually revised directory of sources of financial assistance. It includes not only government programs, but also those offered by foundations, businesses, professional groups, and other organizations.

WHERE TO OBTAIN GOVERNMENT DOCUMENTS

The U.S. government seeks wide dissemination of government documents. Every geographic area has a *designated regional depository* of government documents that receives and retains one copy of each government publication in either printed or microfacsimile form. Distribution is made to libraries by the Office of the Superintendent of Documents. Publications are retained permanently, even after they have ceased to be available from the Superintendent of Documents. Some libraries are designated as "restricted" depositories and are allowed to maintain publications of particular types. Every major metropolitan area has at least one primary regional depository and often has several other restricted depositories. A call to the nearest library is usually sufficient to discover where the regional depository is located. A listing of depository libraries can be ordered from Chief of the Library, Department of Public Documents, U.S. Government Printing Office, Washington, DC 20402. Many libraries that are not designated depositories receive some government publications as well.

In addition, the U.S. Government Printing Office publishes a catalog of documents that includes list prices. Various types of documents are listed in the catalogs, from the statistical reports of the Census Bureau to information pamphlets on various topics. It is generally possible to obtain single copies of many of the shorter publications at no cost. The Government Printing Office also maintains bookstores in a number of large cities throughout the United States.

Although the government provides much information routinely, not all information is disseminated widely. Special studies and reports of agencies may not be released to the general public. Many of these documents are available upon request; however, such requests may need to be made under the Freedom of Information Act.

OBTAINING INFORMATION UNDER
THE FREEDOM OF INFORMATION ACT

An important tool for obtaining documents about the workings of government is the Freedom of Information Act. Any citizen may request copies of a wide array of government reports, memoranda, agency transcripts, and other documents, subject to rather specific limitations. Inspiration for the development of the Freedom of Information Act has strong roots that go back almost to the foundation of our country. In 1822, James Madison said, "A popular government without popular information or the means of acquiring it is but a prologue or farce or a tragedy or perhaps both. Knowledge will forever govern ignorance, and a people who mean to be their own government must arm themselves with the power knowledge gives."

There is nothing difficult about obtaining information under the Freedom of Information Act. One need only identify the information desired in a letter of request. It is not even necessary to state why you need the information. The law requires that an agency receiving a request under the act respond to it in some manner within 10 working days; however, this does not mean that the information will be sent quickly. The Freedom of Information Act is far from foolproof, and different agencies handle requests quite differently. Furthermore, the determination of what constitutes exempted information is left largely to the discretion of administrators. Ironically, in some agencies, documents that might otherwise be more readily available now require a formal request under the Freedom of Information Act.

Many agencies have specified officers who are responsible for information requests. To speed the processing of requests, it usually is wise to write "Freedom of Information Act request" both on top of the request and on the envelope in which it is mailed. The act allows agencies to charge for information, but these charges cannot exceed the actual cost of searching for and copying documents. If the charge is modest or the information was produced for general use, there may be no charge. There are also four circumstances under which you may avoid paying all or some of these charges: if you are indigent; if the information would benefit the general public; if, in making a request, you set a dollar limit or ceiling on costs; or if you ask to examine the documents at the agency rather than purchasing them.

The Freedom of Information Act requires agencies to publish or make available for public inspection several types of information. These include (a) descriptions of agency organization and office addresses; (b) statements of the general course and method of agency operation; (c) rules of procedure and descriptions of forms; (d) substantive rules of general applicability and general policy statements; (e) final opinions made in the adjudication of cases; and (f) administrative staff manuals that affect the public. This information must either be published in the *Federal Register* or be made available for inspection and copying without the formality of a Freedom of Information Act request.

All other records of a federal agency may be requested under the Freedom of Information Act. The Freedom of Information Act, however, does not define what constitutes a "record." Any item containing information that is in the possession, custody, or control of an agency usually is considered to be an agency record under the Freedom of Information Act. Personal notes of agency employees may not be agency records. A document that is not on "record" will not be available under the Freedom of Information Act.

Information produced by Congress (or by congressional agencies, such as the Library of Congress), the Government Printing Office, and the federal judicial system is not covered under the act. Presidential papers are also exempt. Even for agencies to which the act applies, the following nine categories of information are exempt from the act:

1. Classified information on national defense and foreign policy. Government secrets and confidential material also are covered by this provision. Upon receipt of a request, agencies are required to review the information to determine if it should remain classified.

2. Information exempt under other laws (e.g., tax returns) or that is prohibited from release by law.

3. Internal communications, such as intra- and interagency memoranda.

4. Personal and private information such as medical records and personnel files, which, if released, would constitute an invasion of privacy.

5. Information from investigatory files that, if released, would interfere with law enforcement, be an invasion of privacy, expose confidential sources or investigative techniques, endanger a life, or deprive someone of the right to a fair trial.

6. Information about financial institutions (e.g., the Federal Reserve Board).

7. Information about wells, including certain maps.

8. Internal personnel practices and rules that do not involve interests of individuals outside of the agency.

9. Confidential business information. Designed to exempt trade secrets and confidential financial data, this exemption has been the most controversial of the nine. The determination of what does or does not fall under this exemption is unclear and is left largely to the discretion of administrators.

If only a portion of the information requested falls under an exemption, the rest of the material must be released. If a request is denied, the agency involved must provide notification, the reasons for the denial, the names and addresses of those responsible for the denial, and information concerning the appeal process. The right of appeal is guaranteed by the act, although most agencies require that appeals be filed within 30 days of the notification of denial. Appeals are frequently successful; furthermore, court action may be taken if the appeal is denied. More information about the Freedom of Information Act can be obtained from the Freedom of Information Clearinghouse, P.O. Box 19307, Washington, DC 20036.

One problem associated with obtaining information under the Freedom of Information Act is that of knowing what to ask for. According to the act, you must be able to provide a "reasonable" description of the information you want. One approach to this problem is to examine request letters to agencies. These letters, which become part of the public record, often are kept in reading rooms maintained by agencies. Examining requests provides a useful means for identifying what information may be available from a particular agency. A second problem with information requests is one of time. Requests may require several months to fulfill, depending on the nature and amount of the information sought and whether an appeal is necessary. Useful publications related to the Freedom of Information Act include the following:

- *The Freedom of Information Act: What It Is and How to Use It*
  Order this from the Freedom of Information Clearinghouse.
- *A Citizen's Guide on How to Use the Freedom of Information Act and the Privacy Act of 1974 in Requesting Government Documents*
  This volume was compiled by the House Committee on Government Operations. It can be ordered from the Government Printing Office.
- *The Federal Register Index*
  This monthly index is bound into quarterly cumulative indexes. It lists what is available from each federal agency through the Freedom of Information Act, how much it costs, and where it can be purchased or examined. Unfortunately, not all government agencies submit such lists. The index can be ordered from the Government Printing Office.

SUMMARY

The list of information sources above is quite selective. It provides only an introduction to the variety of sources of data available from the government. A useful introduction to the use of government data for problem solving is *A Handbook for Business on the Use of Government Statistics* (May, 1979). Another useful reference is *Understanding Social Statistics* (Lutz, 1983). The latter book describes how statistics are compiled, where they are available, and how they may be used by educators, planners, government, business, and the general public.

EXERCISES

Exercise 4.1: If you were involved in the financial services industry, how would you determine what percentage of individual gross income goes into savings? How would you determine whether this percentage was going up, going down, or remaining the same?

Exercise 4.2: If you were involved in long-range planning for a school district, how would you determine whether adequate classroom space would be available in 5 years? In 10 years?

Exercise 4.3: Select any topic. Determine what federal agencies provide support for research on this topic.

Exercise 4.4: Assume that you are in the business of producing blivets. Blivets are sold to several government agencies, including the Department of Defense and the Department of the Interior. How would you identify opportunities to sell blivets to government agencies?

Exercise 4.5: Is the incidence of larceny increasing in the United States? What about date rape and murder?

5

Syndicated Commercial and Other Nongovernment Sources of Information

Information acquisition and analysis is a large commercial industry. Numerous firms routinely obtain and make available specialized information. Such information includes marketing research studies, single-source data, trade association publications, customized research on particular topics, geodemographic information, and econometric data. These data generally are sold to users, but they often lose their commercial value with time and can be obtained at a modest cost. This chapter introduces some of the more common types of syndicated information, discusses how to use these sources, and offers the advantages and disadvantages of using them.

Many private organizations produce data, reports, and other forms of information. This information ranges from customized applications of data collected by government sources to the results of rather extensive primary data collection efforts. Many firms are in the information business, supplying data and reports on specialized topics to member organizations or client companies. Data from these sources are frequently not free; rather, individuals and organizations pay a fee to obtain the information. Because much of this information may be collected simultaneously, however, the costs of data collection often are shared by all parties. Thus it may be significantly less expensive to use these data sources than to do one's own research.

Much of the proprietary information available in the United States is designed to aid business interests with specific needs. These needs range from tracking the sales of products to learning something about the media habits of people at whom advertising will be directed. Because such information offers a competitive advantage to firms possessing it, access to the data is often restricted. It is not unusual, however, for information to lose its competitive value with time and to become more freely available to students, university faculty members, and other interested persons.

The cost and restricted availability of proprietary data and reports are not the only potential disadvantages of using this type of information.

Data generally are collected with specific objectives in mind and may not be useful for other purposes. Definitions of terms and categories may vary widely across sources, making comparisons difficult or even impossible. The reliability and consistency of data may also vary widely from source to source, necessitating careful scrutiny of the data and the procedures used to obtain it.

Despite these limitations, there are some important advantages to using data from these sources. It is almost always less expensive to obtain information from these sources than it is to do primary research. It also is often possible to use data in ways for which they were not intended originally. Finally, because users are charged for the information, there is an incentive on the part of the information providers to ensure its quality and consistency.

TYPES OF SYNDICATED AND CUSTOMIZED DATA

Two broad classes of proprietary data exist. The first often is referred to as *syndicated data;* the second is known as *customized data*. Whenever information may be useful to multiple users, the costs of obtaining information are high, and the information must be obtained and updated frequently, it is not uncommon for the users involved to pool resources to obtain the information. Trade associations often provide a vehicle for this type of resource pooling. Alternatively, a commercial firm may offer to provide such information to each user for a fee. Generally, with this type of service, the data collection and reporting procedures are standardized. The data are collected on a regular basis and then "syndicated" to various users. The well-known Nielsen ratings of television audiences are an example of one such syndicated service.

As useful as syndicated services are, they often do not answer questions that a specific organization or individual may have. Thus it is often necessary to commission "customized" studies to meet specific information needs. Customized studies may also involve the pooling of resources, but the data usually are collected only once to answer a specific question or set of questions at a particular point in time. For example, a government agency may wish to determine the patterns of usage of its mass transit system. It may either conduct the study itself or commission a private organization to do it.

Many commercial firms provide both standardized (syndicated) and customized research services. Table 5.1 provides a listing of some of the better-known organizations that do demographic research. Some of these firms merely reanalyze Census Bureau data; others offer to collect their own data. The list is not exhaustive, but it does provide a general perspective on the types of data that may be obtained from commercial sources.

In this age of on-line information access, two useful directories are available from Gale Research that provide information on available on-line data bases. These are the *Directory of On-Line Databases* and the *Directory of On-Line Portable Databases*. The latter differs from the former in that the end user may actually purchase the data base, whereas the former lists syndicated data source producers. Another useful guide to customized studies is *FINDEX: The Directory of Market Research Reports, Studies, and Surveys,* published by Cambridge Information Group annually (with midyear supplements) since 1979. This publication lists published, commercially available market, business, and research reports. The most recent edition includes more than 13,500 reports from more than 500 worldwide market research publishers. Although designed primarily as an aid to business researchers, the reports are often useful to others as well. Information on such varied topics as health care, transportation, energy, computers and electronics, media, travel and tourism, and basic industries such as petrochemicals and metals is listed. The name of the organization offering the information is provided, along with an estimated cost of the report. The price of a report may be as much as several thousand dollars; however, many of the publications are available at a modest cost.

The international analogue of *FINDEX* is *Marketsearch: International Directory of Published Market Research,* compiled by the British Overseas Trade Board in collaboration with Arlington Management Publications. This directory lists more than 18,000 studies from more than 100 nations. These studies are classified by product or industry with SIC number cross-references. The service is offered on-line through the publisher (Cambridge Information Group) under the title "Marketsearch Hotline."

Many corporations provide information on a variety of topics. These range from reports to stockholders to descriptions of how products are manufactured and used. For example, Hershey Foods publishes a number of brochures on chocolate that contain information on nutrition, recipes, and related topics. Such investment brokerage houses as Bear Stearns and Merrill Lynch also provide important sources of market information such as industry trends and forecasts. An index to these reports is available through *Corporate and Industry Research Reports*

Text continued on page 83

Table 5.1
Directory of Demographic Data Firms

The Arbitron Company
Arbitron is a marketing information services company providing information on what consumers watch on television, what they listen to on radio, and what they buy in the supermarket. Through an electronic monitoring system called MediaWatch, the company provides information regarding who is advertising to the consumer both on radio and television (network, local, and cable). Arbitron is also able to provide information regarding what kind of consumers are purchasing which products through the use of geodemographics, purchase patterns, and socioeconomic profiles.

Bruskin/Goldring Associates
Bruskin/Goldring Associates specializes in omnibus research services through the use of AIM, an in-home personal interview study that surveys 2,000 adults quarterly. It also offers Omni-Tel surveys, a national survey of 1,000 adults conducted by telephone each weekend. The company recently gained notoriety by conducting an omnibus survey for Hilton Hotels Corporation that revealed that people are more tired when their weekend ends than when it begins.

CACI
CACI provides a full range of demographic and psychographic services, products, and systems, as well as the ACORN market segmentation system, which provides a geodemographic clustering program. Applications include direct mail, consumer profiling, site selection, media planning, and competitor analysis. CACI also provides information on the 1990 U.S. and 1991 U.K. censuses.

Canadian Market Analysis Centre (CMAC)
CMAC provides information on the Canadian market, including demographics for postal codes, cartographic data bases, site reports and maps for retail trade areas, and a geodemographic segmentation system.

Claritas/NPDC
Claritas/NPDC provides demographic data for geographic regions defined by zip codes, school districts, congressional districts, retail trading areas, television markets, and so on. Its newest system is COMPASS, a desktop data-base marketing system that can integrate, analyze, and map out clients' own data, syndicated data, and Claritas/NPDC data bases. The company also offers a life-style cluster system called PRIZM and PRISM +4. The former system classifies neighborhoods into some 40 types based on an analysis of the demographic characteristics of individual zip code areas. The latter system provides profiles based on Zip +4 neighborhoods. Clients can use these classifications to project consumption patterns, target readership or media audiences, or organize direct mail campaigns. Claritas/NPDC also offers profiles of customers based on their use of financial and life insurance products.

Compusearch Market and Social Research Limited
Compusearch offers Canadian census data and its own proprietary data on Canadian demographics and consumer behavior. Consumer expenditure data on more than 1,000 categories are available. The firm provides LIFESTYLES, a geodemographic neighborhood classification system for Canadian provinces.

Computerized Marketing Technologies, Inc. (CMT)
CMT creates and maintains household-level behavioral data bases for consumer marketers in both the United States and Europe. Through use of this data base, marketers can

Table 5.1 Continued

target different messages and incentives to individual households on a solo or cooperative basis.

Datamap

Datamap produces color-coded, custom computer-generated maps for use in trade area analysis and site locations. The firm can combine census and other demographic data with data provided from the organization commissioning the research, such as information from sales slips or credit applications. These data then are plotted in quarter-mile or half-mile quadrants. In addition, Datamap can help clients—for instance, producers of consumer products, marketers, real estate firms, banks, and fast-food restaurants— to develop customer profiles for use in research.

Donnelley Marketing Information Services (DMIS)

DMIS, a Dun & Bradstreet subsidiary, sells demographic studies based on information from its direct mail business combined with data from the census and other public sources. Its CONQUEST marketing information system is personal-computer based, providing access to Donnelley's demographic, economic, and geographic data bases. CONQUEST can analyze the demographic composition, life-style, socioeconomic characteristics, business environment, and propensity of its residents to purchase specific goods and services for 14 standard areas of geography and geometrically defined market areas. DMIS provides information for applications ranging from site evaluation to target marketing, media selection, market analysis, and direct marketing.

Equifax Marketing Decision Systems (EMDS)

EMDS is a provider of integrated products and services for target marketing, direct marketing, and credit marketing applications. The company provides a variety of demographic and marketing information for applications such as target marketing, direct marketing, and credit marketing applications. Products offered include demographic consumer demand, financial and business information reports and diskettes, computer-generated color marketing maps, segmentation systems, and direct mail lists, among others.

Impact Resources

This company profiles more than 288,000 consumers in 49 major U.S. markets across the country, measuring the responses of 5,000 to 18,000 consumers in each market to reflect the reality of the marketplace. Dependent measures collected include demographics, life-styles, shopping patterns, media usage, and retail store preferences.

Information Resources (IRI)

IRI provides a local and national market-scanner tracking service (InfoScan) that reveals a brand's sales performance and provides insights regarding the consumer behavior behind that performance. This is accomplished by integrating scanner panel data from 60,000 households with sales, feature ad, coupon, display, and price data from more than 2,700 stores in 66 markets.

Intelligent Charting, Inc.

Intelligent Charting provides full-color custom maps to assist subscribers in developing, implementing, and managing marketing and sales programs. Their geographic data bases are nationwide, with available geography including zip codes, census tracts, counties, carrier routes, MSAs, DMAs, and ADIs. Custom sales, district, franchise, and market boundaries can be created.

(Continued)

Table 5.1 Continued

Langer Associates, Inc.

This company focuses on qualitative studies of marketing and life-style issues. A full range of services are offered, including focus groups, one-on-one sessions, consulting to corporations on life-styles, and brainstorming for new product generation.

Market Statistics

Market Statistics specializes in using demographic, economic, retail trade, and business-to-business data, all for standard levels of geography and custom sales territories. They also offer a GIS (Geographic Information System) package for site selection and demographic modeling.

Mediamark Research, Inc.

This company provides annual syndicated reports covering national consumer usage of TV, radio, and cable, plus separate reports of 10 top media markets. National cable reports are also available. The company also performs an annual single-source study of media, product, and brand usage and demographics with a sample of 20,000 adults. Finally, the company publishes a variety of reports on different markets, including senior citizens, the affluent, consumer innovators, and those with active life-styles.

Metromail

Metromail provides demographic statistics for small areas based on its mailing lists. It provides for segmented lists on variables such as exact age, estimated income, mail responsiveness, home ownership, presence of children, and length of residence at the individual household level. Services also include list and address enhancements, marketing data bases, modeling, and mail production services.

National Demographics and Lifestyles (NDL)

NDL provides consumer data-base information services designed to assist the client in terms of sales and product planning, advertising, dealer support, direct marketing, sales promotion, and customer service. NDL's data base consists of self-reported product- and purchase-related demographic, geographic, and life-style information collected voluntarily from consumers who complete and return questionnaires packaged in consumer goods. Clients also can use targeted mailing lists from the life-style selector, NDL's 25-million-name consumer list data base. This data base provides more than 70 self-reported demographic and life-style selections from which to choose. The company also offers customized market profile information through OASYS and the Life-style Market Analyst.

NPA Data Services

Provides annually updated economic, demographic, and household data bases based on the census for counties, MSAs, states, census regions, and the United States, detailing population by age (5-year cohorts), sex, race, births, deaths, migration, employment, and earnings by industry and income by type. The company also provides a personal-computer software publication of a population and an economic growth model of the U.S. economy, as well as geographic selections of economic, demographic, household, and construction data bases formatted for PC applications.

Scientific Telephone Samples

This company is a supplier of random-digit telephone samples. These samples are conducted on either a weighted or unweighted basis on almost any type of geographic coverage.

Table 5.1 Continued

SRI International

This company is known for its VALS 2 consumer segmentation program, which is a psychographic system for segmenting American consumers and predicting consumer behavior. VALS 2 can be applied to marketing strategy issues such as consumer behavior, product positioning, and creative and media strategies.

Starch INRA Hooper, Inc.

Starch provides an advertising and editorial readership service that studies more than 50,000 ads per year in more than 100 different publications. The company has a data bank of more than 2 million ads and provides services related to advertising and editorial readership studies, audience readership measurements, and both ballot and impression studies.

Urban Decision Systems, Inc. (UDS)

Urban Decision Systems (UDS) offers census data in a variety of forms, depending on the needs of its clients. The company offers a desktop mapping, decision-support, and GIS system that enables the user to integrate, manipulate, and analyze market information. All that is needed is a PC, Microsoft Windows 3.0, and Microsoft Excel. The system has the capacity to read customer data and merge and compare it with UDS demographic, business, life-style, consumer behavior, retail potential, shopping-center, and other marketing data. The system works at the macro (data at the county level and above), micro (detailed marketing data at all levels of geography), and vertical market (general marketing and industry appreciation data at all levels of geography) levels. Other UDS systems include ONSITE, which produces standard site evaluation and trade area reports, and TELESITE, which is a telephone order service for obtaining UDS reports, maps, and data bases for customer-defined areas.

Woods and Poole Economics, Inc.

This company specializes in detailed long-range demographic and economic predictions to the year 2010 for various counties and metropolitan areas. Forecasts include population by age, sex, and race; employment and earnings by industry; retail sales by kind of business; household data; and personal income by source. The company, upon request, also does special regional market forecasts.

SOURCE: Adapted from Martha Farnsworth Riche (1991), "1991 Directory of Marketing Information Companies," supplement to *American Demographics*.

Index (CIRR) on an annual basis. CIRR provides a microfiche collection of these reports.

Trade associations are also an invaluable source of information. Almost every industry, from grape growing to banking, has one or more trade associations. These associations often sponsor studies that they make available to members and often to outsiders as well. They may also publish or sponsor publication of specialized reports. A significant amount of very detailed information is also available in trade publications. Table 5.2 illustrates a selected number of publications available for just one industry, the beverage industry.

Table 5.2

Selected Trade Publications Relevant to the Beverage Industry

Publication	Content
Beer Marketer's Insights	Broad discussion of current developments in the brewing industry concerning competitive battles, wholesaler relationships, etc.
Beverage Industry	Detailed reporting of developments in key beverage areas, especially soft drinks, bottled water, and noncarbonated drinks
Beverage World	In-depth coverage of leading beverage areas in terms of marketing, production, and packaging
Beverage World Periscope	Trade news for all beverage categories
Bottled Water Reporter	In-depth coverage of the bottled-water category
Brewers Almanac	United States beer industry statistics
Drinks International	Publishes an editorial on all the various drink categories
Impact Annual Beer Market Review and Forecast	Beer, wine, and spirits data and articles
LNA Ad $ Summary	Advertising expenditures totaled by brand
Mixin'	Newsletter of the American Bartenders Association
Modern Brewery Age	Timely discussion of the beer industry
NSDA Sales Survey	National and regional industry statistics
Wine Tidings	Wines and wine-related subjects; food, travel, vintage reports, tastings

There are several useful guides to trade associations. Among these are the *National Trade and Professional Associations of the United States,* the *Encyclopedia of Associations, Trade Directories of the World,* and the *Directory of European Associations.* Many directories also are compiled for specific industries. Two very useful guides to such directories are the *Guide to American Directories,* which lists more than 7,500 trade, professional, and industrial directories, and the *Guide to American Scientific and Technical Directories.*

The number of firms providing syndicated or customized research is far too large to allow a summary of all of them in this chapter. There are, however, several common objectives for commissioning research. Therefore, the remainder of this chapter discusses the most frequent uses of this information by administrators and businesses. This is not to suggest that there are no other uses for these data; indeed, such additional uses will be pointed out as appropriate.

GENERAL INFORMATION ABOUT COMPANIES

A common information requirement of many organizations is information about other organizations. There are a number of very useful guides to commercial organizations in the United States and abroad; several of the better-known examples are listed in Table 5.3. Most of these guides are quite general but describe how to obtain access to additional information. SIC codes (the Standard Industrial Classification codes used by the Census Bureau) are particularly useful, because many other sources list information by SIC code. The identification of the manufacturer(s) of particular products or brands is also extremely helpful. For example, if one needs to research personal computers, these guides will provide a basis for identifying the firms that manufacture them and the associated SIC codes. This information is then the basis for further data collection efforts.

FINANCIAL DATA ON ORGANIZATIONS

Rather detailed financial information is available about many organizations. Not only are Form 10-K reports (the detailed forms filed by corporations, discussed in Chapter 4) available from the SEC, but numerous firms also provide highly specialized information relevant to financial performance in the industry. This information may range from general overviews of the financial performances and activities of a variety of industries to details related to a specific industry. Such information often is used by potential investors, by firms engaged in analyses of competitors, and by researchers in economics, finance, and accounting. The number of publications dealing with financial aspects of organizations is far too large for a comprehensive listing in this chapter. Table 5.4 describes some of the more frequently used publications; the reference librarians of most libraries can provide information about other sources.

MARKETING AND CONSUMER INFORMATION

A wealth of data are available on how people spend their time and money. Such information is particularly valuable to firms engaged in

Table 5.3
Sources of Information About Commercial Organizations

Directory of American Firms Operating in Foreign Countries
Lists more than 3,000 American companies and countries of operation.

Dun & Bradstreet Million Dollar Directory
Lists 160,000 businesses with a net worth of $500,000 or more, including industrial corporations, utilities, transportation companies, bank and trust companies, wholesalers, retailers, and so forth. Available on-line through Dialog Information Services.

Dun's Guide to Israel
A guide to about 8,000 leading Israeli industrial and commercial firms.

Europe's 15,000 Largest Companies
A guide to 8,000 leading industrial companies, 2,500 trading companies, 350 banks, 350 transportation firms, 200 insurance firms, 100 hotels and restaurants, 150 ad agencies, and 250 other firms. Entries include company name, headquarters, contact, International Standard Industrial Classification (ISIC) code, sales, number of employees, number of shareholders, and other operating ratios.

F & S Index to Corporations and Industries, United States (Published by Predicasts, Inc.)
This publication provides information on more than 750 businesses and financial publications. It is probably the best single index for finding current information on U.S. companies and industries. Published weekly, with monthly, quarterly, and annual cumulations, it is indexed by company and SIC code. It is available on-line.

F & S Index, Europe; F & S Index, International
These are both companion volumes to F & S Index, United States. They are published monthly, with quarterly and annual cumulations. Both volumes are indexed by SIC code, region and country, and company. Both are available on-line.

Kelly's Manufacturers and Merchants Directory
A world directory with special emphasis on the United Kingdom. Includes a listing of more than 84,000 British firms.

Marketing Economics Key Plants: Guide to Industrial Purchasing Power
Lists more than 40,000 key manufacturing plants with 100 or more employees. Entries include company name, address, number of employees, phone, and SIC code.

Sheldon's Department Stores
An annual guide to the largest chain and independent retail operations, including department stores, department store chains, home furnishing stores, women's specialty stores, and major women's specialty store chains.

Standard & Poor's Register of Corporations, Directors and Executives
A three-volume guide to more than 50,000 U.S. and Canadian corporations, including names and titles of more than 40,000 officials. Volume 1 provides biographies of 70,000 executives and directors of the corporations. Volume 2 provides an alphabetical listing of corporations, their products, officers, SIC codes, number of employees, and sales figures. Volume 3 indexes companies geographically by SIC code and by corporate family groups.

Thomas Register of American Manufacturers
This publication is a comprehensive guide to American manufacturing. More than 150,000 manufacturing firms are listed. Firms are indexed by company name, product(s) produced, and brand names. Available on-line through Dialog Information Services.

Table 5.3 Continued

Who Owns Whom (North American Edition)
A guide to U.S. and Canadian parent companies, subsidiaries, and associate companies
that includes 6,500 parent companies and 100,000 domestic and foreign subsidiaries
and associated companies. Volumes are also available for Australia and the Far East,
continental Europe, the United Kingdom, and Ireland.

selling products and services, but it is also useful to economists, anthropologists, sociologists, and social psychologists who are interested in the socioeconomic characteristics of a society and its culture. The largest syndicated research services provide information on the public's buying and media habits, life-styles, and attitudes and opinions.

An example of such research can be provided by a discussion of a study conducted by R. H. Bruskin Associates for the Hilton Hotels Corporation. The study was an omnibus telephone survey involving 1,024 interviews across the United States. The study confirmed some key emerging life-style trends in the 1990s, such as more people working, busier schedules, and less time for relaxation and fun. The study revealed that most people start their weekends tired, and by the end of the weekend, very few feel any more energetic than when the weekend began. On average during weekends, people spend about 8 hours less than they would like on relaxing activities and about 6 1/2 more hours than they want doing household chores. This study helped to develop the Hilton marketing strategy known as the "Bounceback Weekend." According to Hilton, the solution to the dilemma of a nonrelaxing weekend with too many chores is to get away. The "Bounceback Weekend" represents a getaway break that allows the guest to relax and recharge after a stressful week. Consistent with the research, Hilton prepared a "guide to bouncing back" that provides helpful hints on how to manage the week so that one *can* get away and get the most relaxation from the weekend.

There are numerous other sources of information about people and organizations. One of the most common sources of such information is the mail panel. Mail panels are composed of households that have agreed to participate in periodic mail surveys. These surveys may ask for attitudes and opinions on political events, plans for purchases in the future, reactions to products or services, or time spent in various activities. Because members of mail panels are generally very cooperative and the costs of collecting the data are shared by many users, mail panels are a relatively inexpensive means of obtaining a great deal of information.

Table 5.4
Sources of Information on Finance Records

Companies and Their Brands
Covers more than 40,000 companies that manufacture, distribute, import, or otherwise market consumer-oriented products. Entries include company name, address, phone, trade name, description and source of information, and so forth.

Direct Marketing in Japan
Covers 80 specialist/nonspecialist direct marketers in Japan. Includes an analysis of the direct marketing industry in Japan and provides profiles and analyses of 18 major specialist/nonspecialist direct marketers.

DiskAmerica on CD-ROM
Cover 10 million businesses. The data are divided into Eastern and Western editions. Data include the company name, address, phone, number of employees, sales, SIC code, and so forth.

Dun's Service Companies
Covers 50,000 service firms with 50 or more employees. Entries include company name, address, number of employees, names and titles of key personnel, lines of business, state in which incorporated, and so forth.

Dow Jones Investor's Handbook
Published annually by Dow Jones and Company, the publication gives daily Dow Jones averages for the current year, monthly closing averages, dividend yield, and price-earnings ratios for more than 10 years. Information on the Dow Jones averages from 1885 to 1970 provides useful historical statistics.

Forbes Report on American Industry Issue
List of approximately 1,150 leading publicly owned corporations. Entries include company name, sales and earnings per share, growth rates, return on capital, debt/equity, current price-earnings ratios, 10-year stock gain, and dividend yield.

Fortune Directory
Provides information on the 500 largest U.S. industrial corporations, 50 largest banks, and 50 largest life insurance, financial, transportation, utility, and retailing companies, including assets, profits, and sales. Appears in the August issue of *Fortune* each year.

Moody's Manuals
Moody's publishes seven manuals each year and provides weekly updates. The manuals include *Bank and Finance* (including insurance, real estate, and investment companies), *Transportation, OTC* (over-the-counter) *Industrial, Municipal and Government, Public Utility,* and *International.* Information provided includes current and historical financial data, securities information, location of the company, a brief history of the company, and the officers of the corporation. Moody's also publishes a *Corporate Profiles Handbook,* a *Quarterly Handbook of Common Stocks,* a *Bond and Record Survey,* a *Global Short Term Market Record,* and an *Unlisted Manual.* Many of these publications are available on-line through Dialog Information Services.

Standard & Poor's Stock Reports
Three separate publications are available, one on the New York Stock Exchange and one on the over-the-counter and regional exchanges. Each report provides brief descriptions of companies, earnings and balance sheet data, capitalizations, and so on.

Table 5.4 Continued

Value Line Investment Survey
A four-volume publication that provides ratings and reports on approximately 1,700 stocks. The set includes the *Value Line Investment Survey, Options and Convertibles, OTC Special Situations, Selection and Opinion,* and other special reports.

SOURCE: Adapted from Charles B. Montner (1991), *Directories in Print* (Detroit, MI: Gale Research, Inc.).

There are, however, some potential dangers in their use (to be covered in greater detail in the next section). First, one can always question whether the people who agree to serve on a panel are different from the population under study. That is, these people may have more leisure time to spend on responding to questionnaires and a significant interest in the topic of focus; the issue then boils down to a potential bias on key dependent measures. A well-known mail panel is the Conference Board Survey of Consumer Confidence. Some universities and not-for-profit organizations also operate mail panels.

A variation of the mail panel is the mail-diary panel. Members of these panels maintain diaries of various activities. Market Research Corporation of America (MRCA) is among the oldest mail-diary panel operations. Approximately 7,500 families throughout the United States provide the MRCA with detailed descriptions of their purchase habits by keeping diaries. They record such information as what was purchased, when and where the purchase was made, how much it cost, the quantity purchased, the number of items in the package, and whether the purchase involved a special deal (or coupon). Each month MRCA provides a report of consumer purchases during the previous month, by product category and brand. The families participating in the diary panel are selected to be representative of the larger population with respect to such characteristics as geography, income, presence of children, family size, age, and education. They are not necessarily representative with respect to other characteristics, however, so some caution must be exercised with respect to broad generalizations about very specific behaviors.

Arbitron is another vendor of diary panels. Its principal concerns are the television and radio listening habits of individuals. People recruited for the Arbitron panel keep diaries of their media habits, and this information is compiled and reported each month. These data also provide the basis for special reports on topics such as changing media habits and media habits of selected subpopulations. As an incentive, people who are asked to participate in the Arbitron radio panel are told that not everyone is asked to participate in the panel, and that their responses are extremely important. As a further incentive, they are sent three crisp dollar bills with a note attached to each dollar: *"Thank You . . . for filling out your diary.* By returning your diary when the survey week ends, you help the broadcasters provide more programs to your liking."

ADVANTAGES AND DISADVANTAGES
OF MAIL PANELS

Mail panels are a cost-effective means for obtaining a great deal of information. Because data are collected continuously, it is possible to track changes over time and thus to conduct quasi experiments. Despite these advantages, there are several drawbacks. First, panel members are volunteers. Selection bias may well be present in these panels, because as few as one in five households contacted agrees to serve on such panels. Also, people drop out of panels, move, or die. The result is that panel membership changes over time. From year to year, panel member turnover may range from 20% to 33%. Therefore, differences over time may reflect only the mortality rate of the sample. In addition, there is little control over who completes the questionnaires. Thus information that might best be obtained from a particular member of the household might be distorted or missed altogether because someone else in the household completed the questionnaire.

Members of mail panels are subject to a variety of testing effects. New members often develop a "social consciousness" that distorts behavior and reports of behavior. Longtime members often become habituated to questionnaires, new products, and so on. Finally, these panels may not be fully representative of the larger population with respect to behavior, opinions, and other characteristics of interest. Although efforts are made to correct these problems by not using data provided by new panel members for a period after recruitment and by rotating old members off the panel, they still represent potential sources of bias. Nevertheless, such panels can provide some useful insights into the attitudes and behavior of individuals.

Special-purpose panels are also available; for example, panels of single persons, physicians, teenagers, and engineers. Obviously, the most relevant and immediate use of panel data is by major corporations that are trying to understand their customers. Many firms, however, will provide access to panel data for social science researchers. A recent variation of consumer panels links consumer-reported information with data that are gathered electronically. Such data generally are referred to as single-source systems.

SINGLE-SOURCE SYSTEMS

Single-source systems directly link consumers' exposure to advertising and promotion with what they buy. They match individual consumer response with the marketing efforts designed to affect that response. The term *single source* was first used in 1966 by the J. Walter Thompson advertising agency in England to describe a research interview operation that recorded the demographics and reading, viewing, and purchasing behavior of panelists. Today, the term refers to data on advertising exposure and subsequent buying behavior by an individual consumer or panel of consumers.

The introduction of the Universal Product Code (UPC) has made it possible to record purchases and other relevant information through the use of a laser scanner that electronically reads a product's bar-coded description, which appears on the package. The advantage of such a device is that it records *actual* purchase behavior in a detailed, accurate, and timely manner and does not depend on the personal diary entries that were the norm for television and in-store audits. Indeed, the use of television audits can be problematic. According to Howard Shimmel (vice president of research and advertising at MTV), the MTV audience was never measured well by diaries.

Teenagers and young adults are impatient, especially when you have programming vehicles such as MTV or CNN where you can zip in for three minutes and catch a video or a newscast, and zip back to a network program. Television meters, unlike diaries, measure readership in seconds. They will catch zip-ins. (Schwartz, 1989, p. 25)

Diaries, which rely on viewers recalling their viewing habits, often fail to capture such short-term viewing. Likewise, diaries rely on consumers' memories of purchases. Scanners capture data at the point of purchase. Hence scanners allow for management's more efficient use of time and provide for greater sophistication for the retailer, particularly in terms of inventory control. Most importantly, scanners allow the decision maker to measure more effectively the link between marketing efforts and consumer behavior with up-to-date information on every item with a UPC code in the store. Thus, aside from registering the purchase of a product, scanner devices can record the price paid, the use of a coupon, information about shelf space, end-of-aisle displays, and use of cooperative advertising. These variables can then be related easily to their impact on item turnover and, ultimately, net contribution and sales. In 1988, it was estimated that more than 10,000 stores had scanner devices, covering approximately 60% of all commodity volume (ACV) in the United States.

Two electronic monitoring tools create the modern single-source system: television meters (which produce somewhat accurate descriptions of who watches television and what they view) and laser scanners (which electronically register the UPC codes on products to produce instantaneous information on sales). A single-source system, by definition, gathers its information from a single panel of respondents who typically inhabit a reasonably self-contained community that is representative of the demographics of the country. This panel is monitored continuously in terms of the advertising and promotion to which it is exposed and in terms of what subsequently is purchased. The panel typically is recruited through the use of coupons or other inducements, and each panel member carries an identification card that is scanned at checkout. This allows a linkage of the household's purchases to previously collected descriptive information about the household as well as promotional and/or advertising exposure. Aside from this inherent advantage, the single-source system can make the data available rather quickly—almost instantaneously.

According to Schwartz (1989), however, there are three major weak points in the single-source systems available today. First, they don't record thousands of marketing messages to which consumers are exposed, because advertising in print, radio, or outdoors is not monitored (with some exceptions). Cigarettes, for example, are promoted by outdoor advertising, public relations firms, and sponsorship of sporting events. Second, scanners do not record all purchases; only packaged goods that carry bar codes are recorded. Finally, not all store types are considered. For example, a huge volume of candy is sold by convenience stores, kiosks, vending machines, and other outlets that do not have scanner systems.

Applications of single-source systems range from the instantaneous determination of how well a promotion is working to sales response to price changes to inventory control and shelf arrangement. The system allows for microsegmentation in that the buying habits of individual shoppers could also potentially be monitored. Through use of this system, an elderly couple could receive coupons for over-the-counter prescriptions, whereas families with babies would be targeted to get coupons for diapers, baby wipes, and baby food. Another application of scanner data was proposed by Michael J. Wolfe, director of product development and applications for SAMI Information Services. Wolfe suggested that a store's scanner sales and promotion data be combined with an array of demographic and factual information about a store. Specifically, Wolfe examined the impact of the density of the Hispanic population on the percentage change of in-store frozen food category sales. He found that a 10% increase in density of this population led to a 4% increase in frozen food meat/fish volume and a 6% decrease in potato volume. It was noted that for manufacturers interested in marketing to this growing demographic group, such information can provide unique insights and benefits, particularly because certain minority groups traditionally have been underrepresented in panel data.

A number of companies have attempted to create national electronically monitored single-source panels. They are Arbitron Ratings Company of New York City; Information Resources, Inc., (IRI) of Chicago; and NPD/Nielsen of Port Washington, New York. Arbitron's single-source system is called ScanAmerica, and it began with 600 households in Denver, Colorado. In the fall of 1991, Arbitron had installed ScanAmerica in households in eight other cities: Atlanta, Chicago, Dallas, Los Angeles, New York, Phoenix, Pittsburgh, and St. Louis. The company planned to expand to a national service of 5,000 households by early 1993. Arbitron households have meters attached to their television sets, and they have scanning "wands" that panelists use at home to record the UPC codes of the products they buy. These panelists also list which newspapers, magazines, and other print media they read. This system has been criticized for requiring that participants be involved actively in entering the data, which introduces variation into the system and is a source of potential error.

IRI was the first entrant into the single-source area in 1979 with BehaviorScan. This system consists of single-source data collection facilities that collect data via UPC-scanning-equipped grocery and drugstores and panels of households whose purchases are linked to the stores (via an electronic ID card that is keyed at the check out). Behavior-Scan has the capability to target television commercials to specific households. The BehaviorScan facilities are used to test consumer promotions, as well as advertising and product introductions. IRI also provides scanner data from a panel of 60,000 households nationally, called InfoScan. This system is able to develop trial-and-repeat measures, buyer demographics and brand loyalty, and so forth. Of the 60,000 panel households, 10,000 households also have television meters.

Nielsen's single-source system is called ScanTrack, which provides weekly data on packaged-goods sales, market share, and retail prices from UPC-scanning-equipped supermarkets (3,000 in 50 markets). In addition, the ScanTrack National Electronic Household Panel expanded to 15,000 households in 1989 (inclusive of 4,200 where television viewing is also measured, and 8,000 with identification cards). This panel collects packaged-goods purchase data via an in-home scanner. The company uses the information generated by identification cards to make market-by-market analysis of promotions; it uses the information from the in-home scanners to analyze advertising effectiveness.

SURVEY SAMPLING

In addition to continuous panels and single-source data, a number of organizations survey the population (or a subset of the population) using systematic sampling. The Survey Research Institute of the University of Michigan conducts a number of ongoing surveys dealing with significant social issues. Data from and reports of these surveys are available to researchers. One of the largest surveys of households is carried out by a commercial firm, Mediamark Research, Inc. (MRI; formerly called Target Group Index, or TGI). Approximately 20,000 households are involved in the interviewing process. The sample is a strict probability sample of the adult population of the continental United States. Cluster sampling is used to identify households for participation in the study. The primary purpose of the MRI survey is to gather information on magazine audiences for use by advertisers. The survey obtains information about demographics, magazine and newspaper readership, product usage, and other selected activities, as well as some data on television and radio audiences. These data then are summarized in a series of volumes that are arranged by magazine readership and product category.

MRI is a convenient source of information about the characteristics of people who engage in certain activities, such as purchasing particular products or stocks, or participating in sports or civic activities. Most advertising agencies have current copies of the MRI annual, and many business school libraries maintain back issues. These back issues provide a useful means for examining trends in behavior over time. The Simmons organization provides similar data and reports.

There are numerous other sources of secondary data that compute information about the behavior of individuals and organizations. These range from opinion-polling organizations to firms that monitor the sales of goods and services. A useful guide to these firms is the *International Directory of Market Research Companies and Services* (the "Green Book"), published annually by the American Marketing Association. This publication lists marketing research firms in the United States and selected foreign countries and describes the services provided by these firms. Also helpful is *Bradford's Directory of Marketing Research Agencies and Management Consultants in the United States and the World.* This directory also provides a description of the services offered by various research firms. Table 5.5 describes several services and illustrates that a variety of services are available. Some of these firms make sample reports and other materials available upon request.

INFORMATION ON FOREIGN COUNTRIES

Another frequent area of interest for both businesses and academic researchers is the foreign arena. Much information is available from foreign governments, the U.S. government, and the United Nations. In addition, there is also a substantial amount of information available from commercial sources. *Statesman's Yearbook* provides brief facts about government, population, education, finance, industries, and the like for each country of the world. *Worldcasts*, published by Predicasts, Inc., includes both short-term and long-term forecasts of economic indicators for specific countries. More than 60,000 forecasts for products and markets in countries outside of the United States are covered. Entries include subject and SIC code, the event being forecast, and the base period. The *CIA World Fact Book,* now available on CD-ROM, includes 248 comprehensive country profiles inclusive of information on geography, climate, natural resources, population, language, labor force, government, membership in organizations, economy, gross national product, inflation rate, unemployment, budget, imports, exports, debt, industrial production, industries, agriculture, and many other variables. *BI-DATA: Printout Summary,* published by Business International Corporation, is a compendium of information on the world with volumes dealing with Asia, China, eastern Europe, Europe, and Latin America. The December issues of the weekly journal *Business International* provide similar data for 132 countries. *Pick's Currency Yearbook* is a

Table 5.5
Commercial Research Services Offering Syndicated and Customized Reports

A. C. Nielsen Company
Nielsen was founded in 1923 and in 1984 became a wholly owned subsidiary of the Dun & Bradstreet Corporation. Nielsen offers a wide range of services from the television rating service to ScanTrack (which provides weekly data on packaged-goods sales, market share, and retail prices from UPC-scanning-equipped supermarkets, of which there are 3,000 in 50 markets). During 1989, Nielsen acquired three European research firms and started Home-Scan in the United Kingdom, which employs hand-held scanners to record purchasing in-home.

Bases Burke Institute
This company provides simulated test marketing services and associated new product analyses to clients, like SOVA (source of volume analysis) and PASS (market segmentation). Until mid-1989, this company was part of the Burke Information Services subsidiary of Control Data Corporation.

Elrick and Lavidge (E & L)
E & L specializes in survey research for consumer products and business-to-business clients. Its field service company, Quick Test Opinion Centers, operates 42 mall interviewing sites plus eight focus group facilities and central telephone interviewing centers. The company plans to launch a customer satisfaction panel and to expand its international operations.

Gallup Organization, Inc.
The grandfather of opinion-polling organizations, Gallup conducts an omnibus national survey every 2 to 4 weeks. Every month, it publishes a newsletter for business executives assessing public attitudes. It also produces numerous special-topic reports.

IMS International
IMS measures consumption of pharmaceutical and other health care products, evaluates physicians' prescribing patterns, and provides services that help pharmaceutical marketers to target the efforts of their sales force. The company provides pharmacy sales reports as well as medical indices, which provide data on the patterns and treatment of diseases based on records of practicing physicians in 40 countries.

Information Resources, Inc. (IRI)
In the United States, the main IRI service is INFOSCAN, which is a packaged-goods market tracking system based on 2,700 supermarkets in 66 local markets. INFOSCAN also provides scanner purchase data from a panel of 60,000 households nationally to develop trial-and-repeat measures, buyer demographics, brand loyalty, and so on. IRI also has the Behavior-Scan system, a single-source data collection system. In 1989, IRI launched DataSaver, a system designed specifically for the analysis of scanner data.

Louis Harris and Associates
Harris is a full-service research firm specializing in highly customized, ad hoc, and syndicated research for government agencies, businesses, and nonprofit organizations. Harris surveys and consulting focus on strategic planning, business-to-business relationships, attitudinal studies, and public policy issues in the fields of health care, telecommunications, banking, insurance, real estate, automobiles, education, urban issues, aging,

Table 5.5 Continued

utilities, computers, and mass transit, among others. Harris also conducts international surveys in 70 countries.

M/A/R/C, Inc.

The company performs custom market research designed specifically to predict new product success and to evaluate and maximize ad copy and media plans. In 1989, M/A/R/C introduced IRIS, a software vehicle through which research projects can be managed to facilitate assimilation of the research environment.

Maritz Marketing Research, Inc.

Maritz specializes in consumer satisfaction measurement and custom market research. The company also does syndicated studies for the automotive and agricultural industries. In 1990, Maritz introduced Entrance, a PC-based relational data base that allows clients access to the complete library of Maritz syndicated automotive studies.

Market Facts, Inc.

This company specializes in custom research for consumer, industrial, and service clients. The company has central telephone centers in three suburban sites outside Chicago, a network of nine shopping mall interviewing sites, a 280,000-household data base, a consumer mail panel, and a controlled store audit facility called Marketest.

MRB Group, Inc.

MRB owns the Simmons Market Research Bureau, which produces the Simmons study of media and markets. This study is based on a sample of more than 19,500 adults and includes information on media use, product and brand use, leisure activities, and VALS life-style and geodemographic segmentation. The custom media studies division of Simmons does custom ad hoc surveys. Cuinona (another part of MRB) is a custom research firm specializing in quantitative methodologies, telephone interviewing, mall intercepts, and retail audit research.

NFO Research, Inc.

NFO boasts a 400,000-household consumer panel representing more than 1 million people. Samples of this panel, categorized by demographics and product ownership, are surveyed by mail and telephone for attitude and usage studies, concept and product tests, and tracking and segmentation studies. In 1989, NFO introduced its 16,000-household Hispanic panel, operated through its Hispanic research center in San Diego.

The NPD Group

NPD is organized into syndicated and custom services divisions. The former provides tracking data bases covering store movement, consumer purchasing, and consumer attitudes/awareness to industries such as toys, apparel, textiles, sporting goods, jewelry, petroleum/automotive, electronics, restaurants, and in-home food consumption. Data are collected through a combination of diary panel, mail panel, traditional audit, point-of-sale computerized audit, and telephone interview. The custom services unit consists primarily of NPD's custom research and marketing models division.

Opinion Research Corporation (ORC)

ORC's Public Opinion Index tracks opinions of the general public, executives, government leaders, the media, and the financial community. It offers numerous reports of special surveys and several special-purpose syndicated services.

Roper Organization

Publishes "Roper Reports" and "Roper Reports Index," which are based on data collected from personal interviews.

useful guide to 112 foreign currencies. Finally, the *Encyclopedia of Geographic Information Sources* describes more than 12,000 business information sources in 150 cities, countries, and regions internationally. Both publications and organizations are listed.

SUMMARY

Commercial sources of information are an invaluable resource. The data provided generally address rather specific issues and problems. Because many firms provide this information at a profit, however, it is sometimes costly relative to government sources. There may also be restrictions on availability. Despite these limitations, the data are generally less costly than would be the case if they were collected directly by the user. Also, as information ages, it often loses its commercial value and becomes more readily accessible. This latter fact is largely unknown to many social scientists, who neglect to seek out commercially available data. Such data are often the least expensive and most reliable means for tracking changes in the social structure and culture.

EXERCISES

Exercise 5.1: What can you learn from commercially available sources about the characteristics of the frequent leisure and business traveler? Develop a separate profile of each of these travelers.

Exercise 5.2: What trade association might provide information about the dietary habits of American adolescents? Are there any trade journals that would provide information on this topic?

Exercise 5.3: Write several of the public opinion-polling organizations for a description of their services. Critique their data collection procedures.

Exercise 5.4: Using whatever secondary sources you can identify, answer the following question: Are Americans replacing a work ethic with a leisure ethic?

Exercise 5.5: Using whatever secondary sources you can identify, answer the following question: Are Americans more concerned about nutrition today than 5 years ago?

Exercise 5.6: What sources of information would you examine when doing a financial analysis of a corporation?

6

Computer-Assisted
Information Acquisition

Much information has been transferred to or indexed on computer systems. These computer systems provide rapid and efficient access to a tremendous volume of information. Exhaustive information searches can often be completed within a few minutes by these systems. This chapter discusses the use of these systems.

The advent of the computer age has created a revolution in information technology. The slow, methodical search through catalogs, directories, guides, and reference volumes is being replaced rapidly by the quick, thorough, and efficient computer search. Instead of spending months digging through libraries to locate information, one needs only a few minutes of computer time. An entire industry of on-line computer information services has developed within the last decade. This industry and its technology are advancing so rapidly that new developments occur weekly. Many users of information have realized quickly that libraries, business firms, government offices, and one's own home computer have the capability to identify an enormous amount of information within a few minutes.

In order to access an on-line data base, you must have access to a device that supports data communications. Hence a terminal equipped for communication through the use of an acoustical coupler or a personal computer with either an external or internal modem and appropriate communications software would suffice. Also required is a telephone that serves as the link between the terminal or computer and the host computer. Once these requirements are met, the main task then becomes identification of the appropriate data base and the information needed to solve the problem at hand. This is no easy task. During the 14-year period from 1975 to 1989, the total number of data-base records has increased by a factor of 95.9 (from 52 million to 5 billion), and data bases themselves have grown by a factor of 15.9 (from 301 to 4,786; Williams, 1990).

The principle behind the use of the computer for information searches is quite simple. One stores information in the computer and references it by key identifiers. For example, it is possible to store the information in the volumes of *Psychological Abstracts* on computer, referenced by key words from the title of each abstract, authors' names, and so on. To request information about a particular subject, one would simply enter relevant key words or names into the computer. The computer then identifies all abstracts related to the topic. For instance, a request for information about learning would produce a listing of all abstracts with the word *learning* in the title (probably several thousand titles).

The key to a successful computer search is the identification of the relevant key words and data bases. Obviously, a word appearing frequently in papers, such as *learning,* will produce an overwhelming list of references, many of which are not actually relevant to the topic of interest. Recognition of this problem has produced computer software that allows the searcher to combine terms, eliminate unwanted categories of information, and carry out hierarchical searches. Boolean logic (a logic derived from set theory that is used for computing combinations) is used to accomplish this end. Figure 6.1 illustrates Boolean operators. For example, two or more key words might be combined using an "AND" statement. When two key words are linked by an AND, both words must appear for the reference to be identified. Going back to the prior example of *learning,* the searcher might quickly narrow down the number of citations found by combining the key term *learning* with the organism of primary interest, say, *mice.* The specification "learning AND mice" identifies only those citations referenced by both key words.

Two other operations used to define the scope of a computer-assisted information search are "OR" and "NOT." The OR statement identifies a citation if it is referenced by either one of the key words. For example, "learning OR conditioning" will identify all citations in which either the term *learning* or the term *conditioning* occurs. The NOT operator ensures that citations referenced by certain key words will not be included, regardless of whether other relevant key words also appear. For example, "learning NOT human" would exclude citations involving human learning; "learning OR conditioning NOT human" would produce references to learning and conditioning studies not in human populations. The NOT operator must be used very carefully, because its use can dramatically restrict the number of citations identified by a search.

Many computer-assisted searches can be carried out interactively. Thus the searcher may begin with a broad category and a large number of key words and gradually narrow the search as needed. Most search algorithms

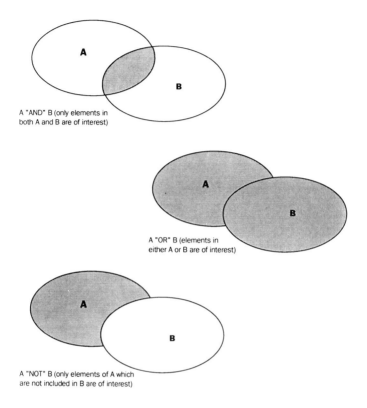

Figure 6.1. Boolean Operators

provide an indication of the number of citations found and allow the examination of the first few citations. If a very large number of citations is produced and many appear inappropriate, further restrictions via AND and NOT commands and by reducing the set of descriptors employed may reduce the volume of output. This hierarchical search procedure may be continued until only those citations desired remain. It may also happen that the citations produced are not at all what is desired. If a search is unsuccessful, it is likely that different key words must be used.

Key words are identified differently depending on the data base. For some data bases, only words appearing in the title are used to reference citations. For others, key words are selected from both the titles and abstracts of citations. A data base called LEXIS, which is used for examining legal issues, actually does word-by-word searches of all citations. Some understanding of a particular data base is necessary to ensure that appropriate citations will be identified by the key words one plans to use. This is extremely important because the *user* and not the librarian is typically the one who accesses the data base today.

Even with the power of the computer, citations may be missed. This may occur because the literature is not in the data base; it may predate the data base, for example. Many data bases do not contain citations prior to 1970. Another problem is that the citation may be in a source that is not included within the data base, or key words may not be appropriate for identifying important sources. Thus it is helpful to do some verification of the results of a computer-assisted search. For instance, one should check that well-known citations related to the area of interest are being picked up in the search. If not, a revision of key words may be necessary. Similarly, because most data bases also allow searches by author, one can double-check by including an author search using a well-known name in the field and seeing if the topic search also picks up these references.

TYPES OF DATA BASES

There are many different types of data bases from many different sources. Indeed, data bases can be classified in many different ways. One approach taken is by form of data representation (Williams, 1990). That is, data bases can be classified as word oriented, number oriented, image oriented, or sound/audio oriented (this is a relatively new phenomenon). Word- and number-oriented data bases can be further subclassified. The former can be categorized into the following main subclasses: bibliographic, patent-trademark, directory, and full text. Numeric data bases can likewise be subdivided into the following main categories: transactional, statistical, time series, and properties. Word-oriented data bases make up approximately 70% of all on-line data bases, with number-oriented data bases making up approximately 26%.

Data-base producers include the government, commercial firms, and not-for-profit organizations, as well as academia. By far, however, commercial firms are the leading producers of on-line data bases, with some estimates as high as 68% of all data bases (Williams, 1990). Commercial vendors of on-line services, such as the Dialog Information Retrieval Service (DIALOG) and the New York Times Information Service (NYTIS), provide descriptions of the data bases they offer. Table 6.1

Text continued on page 109

Table 6.1
Selected On-Line Data Sources

ABI/INFORM (Abstracted Business Information)
1971-present, updated weekly (bibliographic; 417,000 citations)
Provides citations and abstracts of significant articles appearing in more than 800 major business and management journals published worldwide. Available on-line from BRS Information Technologies, among others, and on CD-ROM from the producer.

Accountants' Index
1974-present, updated quarterly (bibliographic; 200,000 records)
Provides citations to worldwide English-language literature in accounting and related business and financial areas as received by the American Institute of Certified Public Accountants (AICPA) library. Available on-line from ORBIT search service.

Advertising and Marketing Intelligence (AMI)
1979-present, updated daily (bibliographic; 250,000 citations)
Provides references and abstracts of advertising and marketing articles appearing in major trade and professional journals. Available on-line through NEXIS.

AGRICOLA
1970-present, updated monthly (bibliographic; 2,500,000 records)
Developed by the National Agricultural Library, this source contains complete bibliographic and cataloging information for all monographs and serials received at the library. Available on-line through BRS Information Technologies, among others.

AIDS Database
1983-present, updated monthly (bibliographic; 6,000 records)
Provides bibliographic citations and abstracts of published materials covering all aspects of acquired immune deficiency syndrome (AIDS), the HCTV-I and -II viruses, and human immunodeficiency viruses. Available on-line through BRS Information Technologies, among others, and on CD-ROM from the producer.

Alcohol Information for Clinicians and Educators Database
1978-present, updated quarterly (bibliographic; 9,000 records)
Contains citations and abstracts of published literature covering all aspects of alcohol use and abuse. Available on-line from BRS Information Technologies.

America: History and Life
1964-present, updated bimonthly (bibliographic; 200,000 records)
Covers United States and Canadian history from prehistory to the present; area studies and history-related topics in the social sciences are included. Available on-line from Dialog Information Services, Inc.

American Statistics Index (ASI)
1973-present, updated monthly (bibliographic; 160,000 records)
Indexes and abstracts all statistical publications issued by U.S. federal government agencies. Covers periodicals, annuals and biennials, series, and special publications. Available on-line from Dialog Information Services, Inc.

BIOSIS Previews
1969-present, updated 4 times per month (bibliographic; 8,000,000 records)
Provides citations to international periodicals and other literature in the life sciences. Available on-line from BRS Information Technologies, among others.

(Continued)

Table 6.1 Continued

Books in Print
1979-present, updated monthly (bibliographic; 1,000,000 records)
Provides comprehensive bibliographic, subject classification, and ordering information
    for nearly 1,000,000 forthcoming books, books in print, and books going out of print.
    Available on-line from BRS Information Technologies and others and on CD-ROM
    from Bowker Electronic Publishing.

Business Tax Report
Updated biweekly (full text)
Reports news and developments concerning tax issues and developments. Available on-
    line from Human Resource Information Network (HRIN).

CA Search
1967-present, updated biweekly (bibliographic; 8,585,000 records)
Contains bibliographic data and *Chemical Abstracts* index entries for documents cited in
    California since 1967. Available on-line from BRS Information Technologies, among
    others.

Chemical Abstracts Service Source Index (CASSI)
1907-present, updated quarterly (bibliographic; 60,000 records)
Contains complete bibliographic descriptions of more than 60,000 serials and nonserials
    monitored by the Chemical Abstracts Service. Available on-line from ORBIT search
    service.

Child Abuse and Neglect
1967-present, updated semiannually (bibliographic; directory; 1,000 records)
Covers publications, programs, research projects, and laws concerning child abuse and
    neglect. Available on-line from Dialog Information Services.

COFFEELINE
1973-present, updated monthly (bibliographic; 20,000 records)
Contains references and abstracts of international journal and other published literature
    covering coffee and the coffee industry, from the farming of coffee plants to its produc-
    tion, packaging, and planting. Available on-line through Dialog Information Services, Inc.

COMPUSTAT (Standard & Poor's Corporation)
Updated on a monthly basis (time series; 420 series)
Provides quarterly, monthly, and annual financial data for 7,000 publicly traded compa-
    nies, 200 industry composites, and more than 3,000 research companies. Available on-
    line from ADP Network Services, Inc., and on CD-ROM from the producer.

Congressional Record
1985-present (full text)
Provides the complete text of the *Congressional Record,* which contains the public pro-
    ceedings of the U.S. Congress. Available on-line from LEXIS.

Dial-a-Fax Directory Assistance
1983-present; updated daily (directory)
Contains information on users of facsimile equipment worldwide. Producer offers search
    services.

Dialog Bluesheets
1988-present; updated weekly (directory; 325 records)
Provides descriptions and guidelines for searching all data bases that are currently accessible
    on-line through DIALOG. Available on-line through Dialog Information Services, Inc.

Table 6.1 Continued

Disclosure Database
1977-present, updated weekly (time series; directory; 12,300 records)
Contains business information and approximately 230 financial data items on more than 12,000 publicly owned companies in the United States whose securities are traded on the New York Stock Exchange, American Exchange, NASDAQ, and OTC. Available on-line from ADP Information Services and on CD-ROM as part of COMPACT DISCLOSURE.

Dissertation Abstracts Online
1861-present, updated monthly (bibliographic; 988,800 records, of which 288,800 contain abstracts)
Provides bibliographic citations to published dissertations accepted by American colleges and universities since 1861. Available on-line from BRS Information Technologies, among others, and on CD-ROM from UMI On-Disc.

Dow-Jones News (DJN)
Covers the most recent 90 days, updated continuously (full text)
Reports up-to-the-minute news concerning business and finance worldwide. Provides coverage as current as 90 seconds. Available on-line from Dow-Jones News/Retrieval.

Drug Info
1968-present, updated quarterly (bibliographic; 5,500 records)
Provides citations and abstracts of journal articles, books, and other materials covering the educational, sociological, and psychological aspects of alcohol and drug use and abuse. Available on-line from BRS Information Technologies, among others.

Economist's Statistics
1800-present (statistical; 2,000 data series)
Provides a variety of international economic and financial time series data. Available on-line from the producer.

Electronic Mail
updated as needed (transactional)
Provides descriptions and price information for retail products of all types. Orders may be placed on-line and are transmitted directly to the merchant for billing. Available on-line from CompuServe Information Service.

ENERGYLINE
1971-present, updated monthly (bibliographic; 80,000 records)
Contains references and abstracts of the world's periodical and other published and unpublished literature dealing with the technical and policy-oriented aspects of energy. Available on-line through Dialog Information Services, among others.

ENVIROLINE
1971-present, updated monthly (bibliographic; 130,000 records)
Provides citations and abstracts of the world's periodical and other published and unpublished literature dealing with technical and policy-oriented environmental topics. Available on-line through Dialog Information Services, among others.

ERIC
1966-present, updated monthly (bibliographic; 636,713 records)
Contains citations and abstracts of education-related literature, involving descriptions of exemplary programs, research and development reports, and related documentary information that can be used in developing more effective educational programs. Available

(Continued)

Table 6.1 Continued

on-line from BRS Information Technologies, among others, and on CD-ROM through
DIALOG OnDisc.

Exceptional Child Education Resources (ECER)
1966-present, updated monthly (bibliographic; 60,000 records)
Provides abstracts and citations to published and unpublished materials covering research,
education, policy, and services for gifted and disabled children. Available on-line
through BRS Information Technologies, among others.

Federal Grants and Contracts Weekly
May 1982-present, updated weekly (full text)
Lists federal grants and contracts available to the educational and management consulting
fields, including contracts awarded and grant and contracting opportunities. Available
on-line through Newsnet, Inc.

Foundation Directory
Updated semiannually (directory)
Provides data on more than 5,100 major foundations with assets of $1,000,000 or more or
total grants of $100,000 or more. Available on-line from Dialog Information Services.

Foundation Grants Index
1973-present, updated bimonthly (directory; 320,000 records)
Provides more than 300,000 actual grant descriptions for grants of $5,000 or more reported
by approximately 500 foundations. Available on-line from Dialog Information Services.

Government Publications Index
1976-present, updated monthly (bibliographic)
Indexes U.S. government publications in all subject areas as covered in the *GPO Monthly
Catalog.* Available on CD-ROM through the producer.

Harvard Business Review Online
1971-present, updated bimonthly (full text; bibliographic; 3,000 records)
Provides abstracting and indexing as well as the complete text of articles published in the
printed *Harvard Business Review.* Available on-line from BRS Information Technologies, among others.

Historical Abstracts (HA)
1973-present, updated bimonthly (bibliographic; 250,000 records)
Provides abstracts and indexing for literature covering countries other than the United
States and Canada in the subject areas of history, the social sciences, and humanities.
Available on-line from Dialog Information Services.

Information Bank Abstracts
(bibliographic; 2,750,000 records)
Provides references and abstracts of current affairs articles appearing in *The New York
Times* and other publications, including general circulation newspapers, international
affairs reviews, business journals, science publications, and other periodicals. Available on-line from NEXIS.

INSPEC
1969 to present, updated monthly (bibliographic; 3,235,000 records)
Contains citations and abstracts of the world's technical literature dealing with physics,
electrical engineering, electronics and telecommunications, control technology, computers and computing, and information technology. Available on-line from BRS Information Technologies, among others.

Table 6.1 Continued

LaserDisclosure
updated weekly (full text; graphic)
Provides exact reproductions of original U.S. Securities and Exchange Commission (SEC)
    filings, including graphs, and photos from the more than 6,000 companies whose secu-
    rities are traded on the American Stock Exchange, New York Stock Exchange, and
    NASDAQ. Available on CD-ROM from the producer.

LEXIS American Bar Association Library
(full text)
Contains the complete text of ABA publications covering tort and insurance law; patent,
    trademark, and copyright law; tax law; and other areas of the law. Available on-line from
    LEXIS.

Management Contents (MC)
1974-present; updated monthly (bibliographic; 270,000 records)
Provides citations and abstracts of current management and business journals covering such
    topics as corporate intelligence, labor relations, market research, and business law. Avail-
    able on-line through BRS Information Technologies, among others.

MEDLINE
1966-present; updated monthly (bibliographic; 5,800,000 records)
Contains references to the world's journal literature covering biomedicine, dentistry, nurs-
    ing, and related topics. Available on-line through BRS Information Technologies and
    on CD-ROM from DIALOG OnDisc, among others.

Mental Health Abstracts
1969-present; updated monthly (bibliographic; 500,000 records)
Provides citations and abstracts of worldwide journal articles, books, research reports,
    program data, and other materials on all aspects of mental health and mental illness.
    Available on-line through Dialog Information Services.

MLA International Bibliography
1964-present, updated monthly (bibliographic; 890,000 citations)
Provides citations of published scholarly works dealing with modern language, literature,
    linguistics, and folklore. Available on-line through Dialog Information Services, among
    others, and on CD-ROM through WILSONDISC.

National Master Specification
Continuously updated (full text)
Provides industry-reviewed, nationally oriented specifications for general, marine, and
    heavy civil engineering construction projects. Available on-line from the producer.

National Newspaper Index
1979-present; updated monthly
Provides references to all articles published in five national newspapers covering
    world affairs, politics, business news, scientific news, and other subjects. Available
    on-line through BRS Information Technologies, among others, and on CD-ROM from
    the producer.

(Continued)

Table 6.1 Continued

The New York Times (NYT)
June 1980-present; updated early (full text)
Contains the complete text of each weekday's final late city edition and the Sunday edition
    of *The New York Times,* a general circulation newspaper reporting local, national, and
    international news. Available on-line through NEXIS.

NTIS Bibliographic Data Base
1964-present; updated weekly (bibliographic; 1,341,600 records)
Contains bibliographic descriptions of government-sponsored research, development, and
    engineering reports, as well as other analyses prepared by government agencies, their
    contractors, or their grantees. Available on-line through BRS Information Technolo-
    gies, among others, and on CD-ROM from DIALOG OnDisc.

ORBIT
updated as needed (directory)
Serves as an index to all data bases currently available on-line through the ORBIT search
    service. Available on-line through the ORBIT search service.

PAIS International
1972-present; updated monthly (bibliographic; 300,000 records)
Provides citations and abstractlike notes of public affairs and public policy literature in
    such areas as business, law, and the social sciences. Available on-line through BRS Infor-
    mation Services and on CD-ROM from the producer.

Pharmaceutical News Index (PNI)
1974-present; updated weekly (bibliographic; 270,000 records)
Provides in-depth indexing of 18 leading pharmaceutical industry newsletters published
    in the United States, Great Britain, and Japan. Available on-line through BRS Informa-
    tion Technologies.

Philosopher's Index
1940-present; updated quarterly (bibliographic; 140,000 records)
Contains citations and abstracts to periodical articles in the field of philosophy and related
    fields. Available on-line through Dialog Information Services.

Pollution Abstracts
1970-present; updated bimonthly (bibliographic; 142,500 records)
Contains references and abstracts of international technical literature dealing with envi-
    ronmental pollution research and related engineering studies. Available on-line through
    BRS Information Technologies, among others.

PRIZM Neighborhood Cluster System (Claritas)
(numeric)
Provides data for the classification of all the residential neighborhoods and communities
    in the United States into 40 homogeneous life-style types or clusters. Available on
    magnetic tape from the producer.

PsycINFO Abstracts
1967 to present; updated monthly (bibliographic; 600,000 records)
Contains citations, nonevaluative summaries, and indexing of the world's literature deal-
    ing with psychology and related fields. Available on-line from BRS Information Tech-
    nologies, among others, and on CD-ROM through Silverplatter Information, Inc.

Table 6.1 Continued

PTS F&S Indices

1972 to present; updated weekly (bibliographic; 3,240,500 records)

Contains brief summaries of periodical and other literature on products, services, industries, companies, international economies, sociopolitical activities, and other worldwide business events. Available on-line through BRS Information Technologies, among others.

SCISEARCH

1974 to present; updated biweekly (bibliographic; 1,720,250 records)

Contains citations to international literature covering the natural, physical, and biomedical sciences. Available on-line from DataStar, among others. Also available on CD-ROM from the producer.

SMARTNAMES Consumer Database

(statistical)

Contains individual and household level information on 122 million consumers for the 50 states. Producer offers search services.

Sociological Abstracts (SA)

1963 to present; updated 5 times per year (bibliographic; 200,000 abstracts)

Provides citations and nonevaluative abstracts of the world's periodical literature in sociology and related disciplines in the social and behavioral sciences. Available on-line from BRS Information Technologies, among others, and on CD-ROM from SilverPlatter Information, Inc.

Space Commerce Bulletin

June 8, 1984 to present; updated biweekly (full text)

Offers business intelligence focusing on all aspects of space commercialization. Available on-line through NewsNet, Inc.

World Food and Drink Report

1989-present; updated weekly (full text)

Provides information on worldwide food and drink legislation, as well as new products and packaging. Includes interviews with key industry figures. Available on-line from NewsNet, Inc.

---

describes a representative set of on-line data bases, although the list is by no means exhaustive. There are numerous highly specialized services available. For example, COFFEELINE provides information relevant to the coffee industry.

The cost of an on-line computer search varies significantly. Royalties are charged for the use of certain proprietary data bases, and of course computer time and other resources are costly. Generally costs will range upward from $150 an hour for commercial customers, but they may be less if the service is provided by a university library or a not-for-profit organization. Because most searches can be completed in 15 to 20 minutes, the cost factor is not highly significant. Indeed, compared to a long, exhaustive manual search, the price of a computer search is a bargain. Almost every university, corporate, or public library subscribes to one or more on-line information services. Individuals can obtain access to many information sources through such services as CompuServe and GEnie.

SOURCES OF RAW DATA

It was noted earlier that certain raw data files are available to researchers. Several guides to these data sources are available. Table 6.2 briefly describes several of these. For example, a guide to computer data bases may be found in the *Datapro Directory of On-Line Services*. This directory lists the nature of the service, prices, applications, type of data base, frequency of updating, and scope of the data coverage. Prior to embarking on a primary research effort, it is important to determine whether useful data are already available. Such data may have been collected for quite different purposes; however, it may be possible to use them in other ways.

Researchers in academic and certain not-for-profit organizations may find the Inter-University Consortium for Political and Social Research a particularly valuable source of data. The consortium is an organization of more than 260 universities and colleges that was established to provide scholars at member universities with raw social science data. The consortium provides access to more than 500 data files, including the following:

- U.S. census data
- Current Population Survey
- Annual Housing Survey
- Panel Survey of Income Dynamics
- Surveys and census data from more than 130 countries other than the United States, including both current and historical data
- Computer tapes of the county and city data book in each locality
- Voting records of U.S. members of Congress and senators from 1789 to the present
- American National Election Study
- General Social Survey, 1972 to 1980
- CBS/*New York Times*, ABC/*Washington Post*, and Harris organization polls

Table 6.2
Guides to Computer Data Files

BLS Machine Readable Data and Tabulating Routines
Describes available data and software routines prepared by the Bureau of Labor Statistics
for distribution to researchers and users of research

Computer-Readable Data Bases: A Directory and Sourcebook (Williams, 1990)
Describes 5,578 international data bases. Probably the most comprehensive directory available, updated approximately every 3 years. Indexed by name, subject, producer, and vendor.*

Database Directory
Provides descriptions of more than 3,000 data bases publicly available in North America. Covers full-text, numeric, property, bibliographic, and referral data bases. Publicly accessible on-line in the United States and Canada. Available on-line from BRS Information Technologies with monthly updates or in print annually from Knowledge Industry Publications, Inc. (KIPI).

Datapro Directory of On-Line Services
Covers more than 900 firms offering on-line services; 2,800 data bases and their producers/vendors; and suppliers of related services. Entries include company name, address, phone number, line of business application, and emphasis.

Directory of Datafiles
Describes all of the Census Bureau's holdings of data and information and how they may be ordered. Abstracts for individual data files are provided with quarterly updates.

Directory of Federal Agency Education Data Tapes
Describes available data on elementary through postsecondary education, including demographic, health and welfare, vital, and human resources statistics.

Directory of On-Line Databases (Cuadra)
Covers more than 4,400 on-line bibliographic and nonbibliographic data bases. Nonbibliographic data bases include referral, numeric, or statistical data bases. Bibliographic data bases include textual, numeric, and full-text data bases. Entries include producer name, on-line organizations through which the data base is available, content, type, frequency of updating, and so forth. Vendors and data bases are listed alphabetically in separate lists. The publication is updated quarterly. It is available on-line through the ORBIT search service, among others.

Directory of On-Line Information Resources
A guide to 600 U.S. and Canadian data bases. Entries include data-base title, price, description, supplier, and producer name and address. This publication is available on a semiannual basis.

Information Industry Directory
Lists approximately 4,600 organizations, systems, and services involved in the production and distribution of information in electronic form. Lists data-base producers and their products, on-line host services, and time-sharing companies, including CD-ROM publishers and service companies. Available on an annual basis from Gale Research.

*From *Computer-Readable Databases*, Eighth Edition, edited by Kathleen Young Marcaccio. Copyright © 1991 by Gale Research Inc. Reproduced by permission of the publisher

- Quality of Employment Survey
- National Longitudinal Survey of Labor Market Experience
- Retirement History Longitudinal Survey
- National Crime Surveys
- More than 40 sets of data on war and foreign policy issues
- 40 data sets related to health issues
- 24 data sets on educational issues

Members of the consortium pay an annual affiliation fee, and with the exception of the U.S. census data, all data are available to them at no extra charge. The consortium's headquarters are at the Center for Political Studies at the University of Michigan.

There are potential pitfalls associated with using data from these sources. First, data are not always transferable from one computer system to another, or if they are, a significant amount of work may be required to convert and reformat the data. Second, not all data bases are documented well; thus it may not be clear how data were collected or coded. Third, data may not be in a form that is optimal for a particular analysis. Levels of aggregation may be inappropriate, classifications may not match particular needs, and available computer software may not be able to operate on the data as they are formatted. Finally, all of the comments in Chapter 2 concerning the evaluation of secondary sources apply to raw data as well. Despite these potential problems and limitations, the use of raw data from secondary sources offers tremendous opportunities. It is often significantly less costly than collecting one's own data. Also, because the developers of the data recognize that the data will be shared, there is an incentive to build in verification checks and to collect data that are useful to a wide range of potential users.

SUMMARY

This chapter provided a review of computer-assisted information acquisition. Initially, an example was given in terms of how to carry out a computer-based literature review efficiently and effectively through the use of Boolean logic. A selected review of existing data bases across various disciplines was provided, with an overview of guides and directories to computer data files. Finally, some sources of raw data were discussed, such as the University of Michigan's Inter-University Consortium for Political and Social Research.

EXERCISES

Exercise 6.1: Identify the on-line computer search capabilities to which you have access. Then design a search strategy for obtaining information concerning a topic of interest. List key words; use AND, OR, and NOT operators when appropriate; and determine how you might verify whether the computer search is reasonably complete.

Exercise 6.2: For the topic selected in Exercise 6.1, determine whether there exist any related data files.

7

CD-ROM Technology

The use of computers for storing and retrieving information and data is no longer restricted to large mainframe machines accessed via modem. The advent of CD-ROM technology has provided a means for storing large amounts of information on compact disks that can be read by personal computers. This chapter describes this new technology and the information sources that are available on it.

Recently one of the authors received the following letter:

Dear Executive:

Welcome to the era of Desktop Marketing!

Not many years ago, buying a list meant calling a list company, getting the counts, and trying to decide what to buy. You paid minimum order charges if the list was small, and had to wait three weeks to get it.

Then came floppy disks. A big improvement—but you still had to decide, up front, what lists to buy. There was no way to really explore a data base, to determine which lists might work. The big corporations could do it . . . but they had million-dollar mainframes and programming staffs to help. The small guy simply couldn't pay—*until now*.

Now the wonder of CD-ROM technology makes it possible for you to put our entire data base of 9.2 million U.S. businesses right on your desk! All you need is a PC and a CD-ROM drive. With our company's product, you can research your markets, generate counts and statistics, preview lists, and make better marketing decisions. Then, once you've decided, simply retrieve the names for your direct mail, telemarketing, or sales campaigns.

Instant access . . . no minimums . . . no waiting . . . and complete control over the lists you select. We've taken the hassle out of marketing to businesses!

The letter above illustrates some of the benefits in using compact disc, read-only memory (CD-ROM) technology over other data sources. CD-ROMs look like the compact discs that have been sold in record stores for the past 5 years, except that instead of containing digitized music, they store data and significant amounts of it. A single CD-ROM can hold approximately 600 megabytes of information (as much as the contents of 1,800 floppy disks) or 250,000-plus pages of text. In order to access the information on a CD-ROM disc, it is necessary to have a CD-ROM drive connected to a personal computer (or access to one available in a public library). These disc drives look like regular compact disc players, with the exception that instead of connecting to the amplifier, they connect through a computer port to the PC. In addition to the disc drive, software especially designed for the CD-ROM disc player is needed to use the information on the disk effectively.

ADVANTAGES IN USING CD-ROM TECHNOLOGY

First of all, CD-ROMs provide quick, accurate, and relatively inexpensive retrieval of information. It is not necessary to search through numerous volumes of books to find the information required. The software included in the disk explains how information can be accessed in seconds. In particular, CD-ROM access of data has specific cost and access-speed advantages over on-line data bases. For the latter, there are typically usage costs that can run up to approximately $300.00 per hour.

For CD-ROM, there are no on-line connect time charges or long-distance telephone charges. One can undertake as many searches as desired with the existing CD without extra expense. The most powerful CD-ROM applications usually are sold by annual subscription or a one-time fee for unlimited data access (a selected producer listing of serials available on CD-ROM is presented in Table 7.1). Typically, the user receives a disc with updated information each week, month, or quarter. Nonsubscription CD-ROM products typically are not so high-powered as those discussed above and are therefore less expensive and aimed at a broader market (e.g., Microsoft's Bookshelf crams into a single disc a dictionary, thesaurus, almanac, and spelling checker, as well as *Bartlett's Familiar Quotations,* the *Chicago Manual of Style,* and a zip code menu). Statpack, also a Microsoft product, allows the same sort of access to reams of demographic, industrial, and economic data, including the *Statistical Abstract of the United States.* Also on CD-ROM is *Grollier's Encyclopedia* (the equivalent of 20 volumes and 30,000 articles). There is also the *Oxford English Dictionary* with 252,000 main entries. Many of these discs are available to the public for less than $400.00.

Another advantage of CD-ROM is that you have better control over the information collected. Through the use of on-screen user interfaces, one can easily select from a menu of possibilities. For example, *Compton's Multimedia Encyclopedia* allows one to choose areas of interest from

Table 7.1
A Selected Producer Listing of Serials Available on CD-ROM

American Psychological Association
Includes: Acid Rain Abstracts; American Men and Women of Science—Physical and Biological Sciences; Books in Print; CAD-CAM Abstracts; Energy Information Abstracts; Environment Abstracts; Psychological Abstracts; Ulrich's International Periodicals Directory; among others

R. R. Bowker
Includes: American Library Directory; Artificial Intelligence Abstracts; Directory of American Research and Technology; Robotics Abstracts; among others

BRS Software
Includes: Index Medicus, Index to Dental Literature; Index to U.S. Government Periodicals; International Nursing Index

Congressional Information Service (CIS)
This company has three products available on CD-ROM. Congressional Masterfile 1 allows the user to search instantly the CIS U.S. Congressional Committee Hearings Index (1833-1969); the CIS U.S. Serial Set Index (1789-1969); the CIS U.S. Congressional Committee Prints Index (1830-1969) and the CIS Unpublished U.S. Senate Committee Hearings Index (1823-1964). Masterfile 2 presents the CIS Index from 1970 to the present. The Statistical Masterfile includes the American Statistics Index, the Statistical Reference Index and the Index to International Statistics.

Dialog Information Services
Includes: Canadian Business Index; Engineering Index Monthly and Annual; Index Medicus; Index to Dental Literature; International Nursing Index; NTIS Bibliographic Data Base; Thomas Register of American Manufacturers

Disclosure Information Service
Disclosure has a CD-ROM product available called Compact D/SEC. This product gives the user access to detailed information on more than 12,000 public corporations whose securities are traded on the New York Stock Exchange, the American Stock Exchange, or the NASDAQ or OTC exchanges. Data are extracted and abstracted from documents whose companies must regularly file with the Securities and Exchange Commission (SEC). This service is available via annual subscription, with monthly updates. Each disc contains, complete profiles for each company, annual (5-year comparative) balance sheets and income statements, annual cash flow statements (up to 3 years), quarterly financial reports (up to six quarters), 5-year summary and 5-year growth rates for net income, sales and earnings per share (EPS), and so forth.

Dun's Marketing Services, Inc.
In August of 1989, Dun's announced that its *Million Dollar Directory* was available on CD-ROM. This gives the user the capability to access the full company records of 180,000 corporations in the United States and more than 500,000 biographies of corporate executives. Only corporate headquarters with more than $500,000 in revenue are included in the directory.

Institute for Scientific Information
The product includes the Social Science Citation Index.

Table 7.1 Continued

Moody's
Moody's has three main products on CD-ROM. *Moody's 5000* gives the user complete information on all New York Stock Exchange, American Stock Exchange, and OTC National Market System (NMS) companies. *Moody's OTC Plus* provides information on more than 3,500 companies traded on NASDAQ or OTC. Finally, *Moody's International Plus* provides access to more than 5,000 non-U.S.-based companies operating in more than 100 countries.

OCLC
Includes: Current Index to Journal in Education; NTIS Bibliographic Data Base; Selected Water Resources Abstracts

SilverPlatter Information, Inc.
Includes: Bibliography of Agriculture; Biological Abstracts; Cumulative Index to Journals in Education (ERIC); Index Medicus (Medline); Monthly Catalog of U.S. Government Publications; NTIS Bibliographic Data Base; Peterson's Guide to Graduate Professional Programs: An Overview; Population Index; Sociological Abstracts; Yearbook of Cardiology; Yearbook of Oncology; among others

Standard and Poor's Compustat PC Plus
Compustat data bases of more than 12,000 companies are merged on a single CD-ROM along with precalculated ratios and growth rates, geographic data, earnings estimates, a descriptive list of SIC codes, principal officers, and address. PC Plus allows the user to work with the data easily and screen variables, time periods, or across data bases (i.e., companies, segments, or industries).

W. W. Wilson
Includes: Applied Science and Technology Index; Biography Index; General Science Index; Humanities Index; Index to Legal Periodicals; Index to U.S. Government Periodicals; Monthly Catalog of the United States Government Publications; Readers Guide Abstracts; Social Sciences Index; among others

---

among Idea Search, Title Finder, World Atlas, Science Feature Articles, and Researcher's Assistant. More specific submenus within each of these more general menus provide further assistance in searching the disk until the relevant information is accessed. *Business Lists-on-Disc* allows subscribers to access businesses based on characteristics related to type of business (Yellow Pages headings or SIC codes); number of employees; franchise, brand, or professional specialty; geographic area; and company name.

The information on a CD-ROM cannot be changed, accidentally or otherwise, and hence leads to lower failure rates compared to floppy disks and some semblance of data permanence. Because the information is stored on an aluminized plastic disk, it is safe from magnetic fields and coffee spills and is insulated somewhat from baby's and Rover's teeth. Finally, CD-ROMs can be updated expeditiously; all that is involved is the taking of a new imprint of the data base containing every file. Users throw away the old CD-ROM and use the updated version.

LIMITATIONS OF CD-ROM TECHNOLOGY

Although the storage of information in CD-ROM format has many advantages, there are some limitations that should be noted. First, to use this new technology, a CD-ROM drive is required. These drives are manufactured by such companies as Sony, Chinon, Denon, and Hitachi at a cost of around $300 to $800. In addition, as noted earlier, one also needs software specifically designed for his or her CD-ROM player to access the information on the disc. It may take an investment of time to learn how to use such retrieval software effectively. Second, in some instances, the data on the disc may not be as up-to-date as those found on an on-line system (although CD-ROM data bases are updated on a regular basis). Finally, the data you need simply may not be available in an electronic format on CD-ROM.

CD-ROM APPLICATIONS

The most popular CD-ROM applications are those in which it is either necessary to distribute or access large quantities of information. The discussion presented at the beginning of this chapter illustrated the data-access advantages of CD-ROM; however, using this technology to distribute information can also lead to significant cost savings. For example, consider the cost of sending out a large report to numerous clients. Although the CD-ROM master disc for the report could cost about $1,500 to produce, each additional disc typically can be pressed for about $2.00. Depending upon the number of copies of the report needed, the cost of the paper, photocopying, labor, and postage may quickly outweigh the cost of the disc. Using a specific example, in recent years, Mack Truck, Inc., has converted 875,000 pages of illustrated parts lists to the CD-ROM format for dealers around the world. Trial runs reported that experienced counter staff took an average of 14 minutes to find 10 parts in printed manuals, whereas inexperienced staff using the CD-ROM approach found the same parts in an average of 90 seconds—an almost tenfold gain in efficiency.

There are now more than 500 CD-ROM data bases available to support a wide range of business and professional needs. Even the U.S. government has gotten into the act, as the 1990 population census is slated to be available on CD-ROM in the near future, and both the 1982 Census of Retail Trade and 1982 Census of Agriculture are currently available in this format. CD-ROM data bases have broad application, such as helping a physician diagnose an illness or assisting a lawyer in legal research. Approximately one third (36%) of CD-ROM data bases are related to law, medicine, or business, 34% fall within the science and technology category, 27% are classified as general, and 3% are representative of the arts and humanities. Using the research findings and categorization scheme of data bases as source, indexes, or reference (proposed by Nichols & Van Den Elshout, 1990), many currently available products (45%) can be classified as source data bases containing full-text or numeric data, computer software, images or sound, maps and charts, and dictionaries and encyclopedias. Examples of source data bases on CD-ROM include the *CIA World Fact Book; CMC Medical Yearbook;* the Real Estate Transfer Database; the Census of Agriculture and Census Bureau Disc; and SilverPlatter's DiscAmerica and the World Weather Disc (see Table 7.2).

Index data bases constitute 31% of CD-ROMs and consist of bibliographic records, journal articles, monographs, and other forms of publications (including library catalogs and data bases of MARC records). Examples of indexes include SilverPlatter's AIDSline, ERIC, Medline Professional, AV Online, the CD Music Guide, and Nursing InDisc (see Table 7.2). Finally, reference data bases make up 24% of available CD-ROMs. They include directories (city, telephone, "who's who," and other types) as well as catalogs of nonbibliographic items. Examples include *Compton's Multimedia Encyclopedia, McGraw-Hill's Science and Technical Reference Set*, the National Directory, PhoneDisc USA, the Reference Library, and *Peterson's College Database* (see Table 7.2).

SUMMARY

The many advantages of using CD-ROM data bases were discussed. Specifically, they provide quick, accurate, and relatively inexpensive retrieval of information; better control over the information collected; and safer storage of data (i.e., lower failure rates). It was noted that the use of this technology requires an investment of time and money both

Table 7.2
Selected Data Bases Available on CD-ROM

Source Data Bases

Census of Agriculture

Presents data from the 1987 census, with more than 3,000 data items from each U.S. county focusing exclusively on agriculture.

Census Bureau Disc

Presents data from the 1982 censuses of retail trade and agriculture, formatted in dBase III.

CIA World Fact Book

Included are 248 comprehensive country profiles, with details on geography, maritime claims, climate, terrain, natural resources, land use, population, language, literacy, natural resources, GNP, inflation rate, unemployment, exports, imports, and so forth. For example, from this product one can ascertain that Kuwait has a land area that is slightly smaller than that of New Jersey. Its climate is that of a dry desert, with intensely hot summers and short, cool winters. Iraq had 2,193,448 males aged 15 through 49 fit for military service in 1989, and 212,318 on average reach military age annually.

CMC Medical Yearbook

Includes the full text of 12 medical yearbooks, including the *Yearbook of Cardiology* and the *Yearbook of Oncology*.

Real Estate Transfer Database

Contains 8 years of Massachusetts and Connecticut real estate transactions, including more than 500,000 individual records and more than 1,000,000 names. Data are classified according to buyer name, unit destination, county, mortgage amount, seller name, condo unit, and so forth. Every real estate transfer with a value of more than $1,000 is included, so that one can easily track the movement of properties to find buyers, sellers, prices, and mortgages.

SilverPlatter's DiscAmerica

Provides a residential directory of names for more than 80 million residences across America. Included are complete addresses, zip codes, and phone numbers, as well as dwelling size and length of residence.

TIGER/Line

Presents an extract of selected geographic and cartographic information from the TIGER data base.

World Weather Disc

A massive meteorological data base that describes the climate of the earth today and during the past few hundred years.

Index Data Bases

AV Online

Provides an index of audiovisual materials from the National Information Center for Educational Media: covers, videotapes, films, audiocassettes, filmstrips, and others. More than 320,000 items are indexed.

CD Music Guide

Lists more than 50,000 recording titles, plus music reviews and articles about various CDs. If you are conducting a search for a particular recording, you can do so by selecting the name of the composer or performer, title of the disc, artist featured on the disc, and/or disc number issued by the record label.

Table 7.2 Continued

Nursing InDisc

Includes 26 years of nursing references (more than 200,000 total) from 517 journals in 24 languages. Application is straightforward to a wide range of patient care including nursing and research.

SilverPlatter's AIDSline

Provides comprehensive and timely information on the AIDS disease. The data base consists of relevant abstracts and citations from several data bases from the National Library of Medicine, including Medline, Health Planning and Administration, and Cancerlit. More than 3,000 journals are surveyed.

SilverPlatter's ERIC

This is a bibliographic data base covering journal and technical literature in the education field. The ERIC data base consists of *Resources in Education* (RIE), covering document literature, and *Current Index to Journals in Education* (CIJE), accessing more than 775 periodicals.

SilverPlatter's Medline Professional

A bibliographic data base for the practicing clinician. It focuses on clinical Medline, including more than 320 journals such as *Abridged Index Medicus,* the *Brandon-Hill List,* and the *Library for Internist List.*

Reference Data Bases

Compton's Multimedia Encyclopedia

Features the entire 8,874,000-word *Compton's Encyclopedia.* It includes more than 15,000 illustrations, including an estimated 5,000 high-resolution charts and diagrams and more than 4,000 full-color illustrations and maps.

McGraw-Hill's Science and Technical Reference Set

Includes the McGraw-Hill concise encyclopedia and the dictionary of scientific and technical terms. The former contains more than 7,300 signed articles, covering all aspects of science and technology from astronomy to zoology. The latter includes 98,500 terms and 115,500 definitions selected and reviewed by authorities in specialized fields.

National Directory

This is a comprehensive listing of important addresses, telephone, fax, and telex numbers in the United States and the world. It is a compendium of key listings in business, industry, and government, with more than 120,000 entries accessed by names and addresses, SIC codes, area codes, zip codes, and telephone area prefixes.

Peterson's College Database

This data base contains more than 3,000 profiles of all accredited, baccalaureate, and associate degree-granting colleges in the United States and Canada. Each profile provides data on enrollment, ethnic/geographic mix, SAT score ranges, admission expenses, financial aid, housing, and so forth.

PhoneDisc USA

This is essentially a computer-based telephone directory with listings covering the entire United States. With an average access time of 10 seconds, numbers can be retrieved by entering all or part of a person's name. The user has the luxury to limit the search to display only listings in selected area codes, zip codes, cities, or streets.

(Continued)

Table 7.2 Continued

Reference Library
Includes on one disc the full text of the following publications: *Webster's Dictionary and Thesaurus; New York Public Library Desk Reference; 20th Century History Guide; Business Forms;* and *Webster's New World Dictionary of Quotable Definitions.*

in terms of purchasing the necessary CD-ROM drive and learning the required software in order to access the information stored on the disc. The most popular CD-ROM applications were described as those in which it is necessary either to distribute or to access large quantities of information. Selected producer listings of serials available on CD-ROM were included, as well as a few of the more than 500 data bases currently available.

EXERCISES

Exercise 7.1: Familiarize yourself with CD-ROM technology by going to your local library to examine what CD-ROM titles are available. Conduct an extensive search in CD-ROM in an area of interest using the titles most appropriate to your area of interest.

Exercise 7.2: Conduct an experiment to determine the efficiency of CD-ROM versus a manual library search by randomly selecting 10 bits of information available both in hard copy and on disk. Note the time needed to access the information using both techniques.

8

Secondary Research in Practice

This chapter provides two extended examples of the use of secondary information for specific problems. One illustrates a typical academic research situation; the second illustrates the solution to a common industry problem.

The first seven chapters have dealt with secondary sources, the evaluation of information, and opportunities for obtaining data. Much of this material has, of necessity, been rather general and abstract. In this chapter, two brief but concrete examples of the use of secondary sources are presented. The examples are not intended to be definitive or representative of all applications of secondary research, but they do provide a flavor of the nature of the task.

EXAMPLE 1: COMMERCIAL PRACTICES AMONG RURAL INHABITANTS OF CENTRAL AMERICA

An anthropologist at a large state university was interested in the trade practices of modern preindustrialized peoples and how these practices compared to those in industrialized societies. Of particular interest was Central America, because the anthropologist had done work previously in the area, had some familiarity with the customs of the people, and spoke the language. Because the anthropologist planned to write a grant proposal for support of travel to study rural tribes in Central America, she had two information needs. First, she had to identify potential sources of research support. Second, she needed to do a literature review in support of her grant proposal.

The researcher began the search for sources of research support with the *Annual Register of Grant Support*. Checking the subject index under *anthropology* and *Latin America,* the researcher identified several potential sources of funding. Among these sources were the Wenner-Gren Foundation for Anthropological Research, Inc., the National Science Foundation, and the National Endowment for the Humanities. A brief letter of inquiry was addressed to each of these organizations, and the anthropologist turned her attention to the literature review.

The information search for the literature review was carried out electronically using IQuest, an on-line information access service offered through CompuServe. This service provides a key-word search of multiple data bases and provides real-time assistance in selecting the most appropriate data bases for the type of information sought. The researcher began the search by combining *rural* and *Central America.* This combination of terms produced matches in *Dissertation Abstracts* and in *Sociological Abstracts.*

The researcher also used the key words *commerce, trade, economics,* and *marketing* in combination with the term *Central America.* To ensure that only works related to contemporary peoples were obtained in the search, she also used the NOT operator: NOT ancient, precolonial, colonial. Finally, the anthropologist searched using the name of a prominent Central American tribe, the Quiche.

In less than 15 minutes, the search was completed, and the researcher had ordered reprints of abstracts or full-text versions of papers of interest. In addition, she immediately printed the abstracts of several papers that appeared particularly relevant.

While waiting for her papers to arrive by mail, the researcher continued searching other sources. In her university library she examined several published indices of the anthropological literature: *Abstracts in Anthropology, Anthropological Literature*, and the *International Bibliography of Social and Cultural Anthropology.* Under the names of various Indian tribes and the subjects of Central America, commerce, and trade, the researcher found a number of potentially relevant publications. At this point, the anthropologist had the names of prominent authors in the field and decided to use the *Social Science Citation Index* to determine whether other papers had cited these particular authors' works.

Finally, the researcher consulted the reference librarian to determine whether she might have missed some important sources. The reference librarian suggested that she examine several publications of Redgrave Publishing Company: *Anthropology in Use: A Bibliographic Chronology of the Development of Applied Anthropology; Anthropological Bibliographies: A Selected Guide;* and *Serial Publications in Anthropology.* In addition, the librarian recommended examining two volumes related to Latin American studies: *Handbook of Latin American Studies* and *Hispanic American Periodicals Index.* These sources yielded references that had not been identified by approaching the literature from an anthropological starting point.

The researcher received the abstracts and papers she had ordered within the week, and coupled with the other sources she had identified, she found that she had sufficient information to proceed with the development of her literature review.

EXAMPLE 2:
A HEALTH MAINTENANCE ORGANIZATION

An insurance company that offered a health maintenance organization (HMO) as a part of its product offerings sought to identify trends and innovations in the industry. A research analyst in the organization was assigned the task of preparing a report for senior management. The report was due in 2 weeks, so primary research was not practical. The analyst proceeded to the corporate library and consulted the reference librarian for sources of information about the health care industry in general and, more specifically, health maintenance organizations. The reference librarian suggested that the search begin with an electronic data base.

The reference librarian accessed one of the on-line computer information data bases, Dialog Information Services. FINDEX was the first source of information consulted. FINDEX is a catalog of market research studies that are available for purchase. Several commercially available publications identified by FINDEX appeared particularly promising:

Medical and Health Care Marketplace Guide, 1990, published by Theta Corporation in Middlefield, CT;

HMO Industry, 1990, published by the *Wall Street Journal*; and

Future of Health Care Delivery in America, 1990, published by Bernstein Research in New York City.

A number of older reports were also identified. Also searched was the Health Planning and Administration data base, which is maintained by the National Library of Medicine. This computer search retrieved more than 200 references to HMOs for which the analyst had abstracts printed.

A third search was carried out on the Industry Data Sources Database, which is compiled by Information Access Company in Belmont, CA, and accessible through DIALOG. This search identified a number of reports on HMOs that were published by consulting firms, including two industry reports compiled by Frost and Sullivan, Inc., of New York

City. One report was published in 1984; the other was published in 1985. This data base also provided the SIC codes for the health care industry in general (800010) and the specific code for HMOs (80001304).

Finally, the Predicasts Marketing and Advertising Reference Service was examined via DIALOG. This data base identified a number of publications dealing with marketing and advertising trends among HMOs. Among these publications were the following:

"Group Health 'Options' Showing Potential of Market-Responsive HMO/ Indemnity Hybrid," *Health Care Marketing*, May 1991, pp. 8-10;

"Inpatient Utilization Trends," *Research Alert*, Jan. 18, 1991; and

"Quirky Promotion Makes Wellness Fun," *Health Care Marketing*, April 1991, pp. 18-19.

The analyst also consulted a number of sources to which the library subscribed. Among these sources were the *Business Index* and the *Business Periodicals Index*. There were numerous papers listed under the heading of "Health Maintenance Organization." The *U.S. Industrial Outlook* also provided a discussion of HMOs under the chapter on health and medical services. In addition to providing information on growth rates, several references were provided, including several government publications.

Finally, the analyst consulted *Abstracts of Health Care Management Studies* and *Abstracts of Hospital Management Studies*, identifying still more source material, including *Group and IPA HMOs;* a 10-year history of the Harvard Community Plan, one of the earliest HMOs; *Finance and Marketing in the Nation's Group HMOs*, published by the Group Health Association of America; and several papers in health administration journals.

Because the analyst had exhausted the sources already known to him, as well as those suggested by the reference librarian, the next stop in the search for information was *Statistics Sources*. This directory of directories suggested that health and medical associations might be identified by consulting the *Encyclopedia of Associations*. A number of additional source documents, primarily government reports, consequently were identified. Among the associations listed in the encyclopedia was the National Association of Employers on Health Care Alternatives (NAEHCA), formerly the National Association of Health Maintenance Organizations. This organization is made up of corporations concerned with health care programs for employees. Among its publications is an annual survey of HMOs. A call to the organization produced a copy of

the most recent survey and several additional helpful sources of information. The NAEHCA suggested contacting the American Hospital Association and consulting the *Insurance Periodicals Index* for additional
information. From the American Hospital Association, the analyst obtained the *American Hospital Association Guide to the Health Care Field*.
The *Insurance Periodicals Index* provided numerous additional references, including the following:

> "Despite Profits, HMOs Find No Joy in Mudville," *National Underwriter:
> Life and Health/Financial Services,* Oct. 29, 1991, p. 34;
>
> "California Still HMO Hotbed as Pru Moves in With HMO Plan," *National
> Underwriter: Life and Health/Financial Services,* Sept. 10, 1990, p. 42; and
>
> "Sears Replaces Indemnity Plan With New HMO Option," *American Medical
> News*, May 6, 1991, p. 11.

By this point in the analyst's search, there was a tremendous amount
of information available for the report. The analyst had identified principle trade organizations, relevant academic and trade publications, forecasts for the industry, primary competitors in the field, and government
regulations relevant to the industry. The analyst then proceeded to summarize the information and write the assigned report. The report was
well received, the analyst was named assistant to the products planning
director, and was henceforth recognized as the corporate expert on
HMOs.

9

Using and Integrating Secondary Information

Even when information on a topic is readily available, it is often necessary to integrate data from numerous sources in order to answer specific questions. This chapter discusses conceptual and statistical issues related to the integration and synthesis of information.

Identifying information relevant to a particular topic is only the first step in using secondary sources. It is easy to become overwhelmed by information. Finding order in a plethora of information is often difficult, particularly when there are inconsistencies, omissions, and differences in methods among various sources. As an example, Aaker and Day (1990) note a limitation in the use of single-source data in that there are "significant differences in results between competing single-source services that raise questions about the quality of the findings" (p.145). Indeed, a common problem faced by researchers using secondary data is that of combining the findings and conclusions of several sources of information. The synthesis of information from multiple sources is an important skill, a skill that until 15 years ago suffered the criticism that it lacked objectivity (Glass, 1976). Furthermore, many users of secondary sources often come away from their efforts frustrated because they could not answer a specific question. In this chapter, information integration will be the focus. Two specific issues will be addressed: how to use existing information to answer questions for which no directly accessible answer exists, and how to incorporate secondary information into a more general research framework.

GENERATING ANSWERS FROM SECONDARY DATA

Answers to specific questions are frequently unavailable in secondary sources, although it is often possible to piece together such answers. For many questions and decisions, a ballpark figure is all that is necessary, and the creative use of existing information can often provide such estimates. Consider one of the most common questions facing organizations, the market potential question: Are there enough people (organizations) interested in our product (service) to justify our providing it? Businesses ask this question about new products, universities ask it about new programs, and government administrators often ask it about new services. Frequently this question can be phrased as follows: Is the demand at least of size X?

Consider the following illustration. In the mid-1970s, a major corporation was interested in the demand for a pet food that included both moist chunks and hard, dry chunks. No such product existed at the time. Therefore, was there currently a significant number of persons who mixed moist or canned dog food with dry dog food? At this early stage in the exploration of this product concept, the firm did not want to expend funds for primary research. Though an actual survey of pet owners would have yielded the best answer, such a survey would have required the expenditure of several thousands of dollars. In addition, further development of the idea would have required a delay of several weeks to obtain the survey results. An effort to develop an acceptable first answer to the question of demand using secondary sources was initiated.

The firm identified the following information:

1. From published literature on veterinary medicine, the firm identified the amount (in ounces) of food required to feed a dog each day by type of food (dry, semimoist, moist), age, size, and type of dog.

2. From an existing survey conducted annually by the firm's advertising agency, the firm obtained information on
   a. the percentage of U.S. households owning dogs;
   b. the number, sizes, and types of dogs owned by each household in the survey;
   c. the type(s) of dog food fed to the dogs; and
   d. the frequency of use of various types of dog food.

It was assumed that dog owners who reported feeding their dogs two or more different types of dog food each day were good prospects for a product that provided premixed moist and dry dog food. Combining the information in the survey with the information from the literature on veterinary medicine and doing some simple multiplication produced a demand figure for the product concept. The demand exceeded 20% of the total volume of dog food sales, a figure sufficiently large to justify proceeding with product development and testing.

As in the above example, it is often necessary to make some assumptions in order to use secondary data. Such assumptions are often reasonable, and by altering the underlying assumptions it is frequently possible to determine how sensitive a particular conclusion is to variations in them. Such sensitivity analysis can be very useful in that it may demonstrate the need for better information or increase confidence in the initial conclusion. For example, in the illustration above, altering the assumption regarding the number of owners who were good prospects for the new product to include as few as one-tenth of the original number did not alter the decision to proceed with the product. Under such circumstances, the value of additional information would be quite small.

USING EXISTING INFORMATION
FOR PLANNING PRIMARY RESEARCH

In many cases, it is necessary to carry out new primary research, because existing information is inadequate for the purpose at hand. Under such circumstances, secondary information may still be quite useful for generating testable hypotheses, estimating base rates, developing a priori probability statements, and designing measurement instruments and sampling plans.

It is often possible to build on previous work when designing primary research. For example, prior work often provides examples of measurement instruments. These instruments, with modification where appropriate, may be incorporated into a new research project. It is not uncommon for questionnaire and test items to be borrowed from existing literature. This not only reduces the work required to develop a new research instrument, but also allows for greater comparability between previous research and the new study. Specific test items and questions are in the public domain and cannot by copyrighted, although entire questionnaires and tests may be. It is customary to cite the source of borrowed items, even when the items are not protected by law. When entire instruments are used, permission frequently must be obtained from the author(s).

Prior research may also be useful for obtaining maximal efficiencies in sample designs. The sample size (number of observations) needed for a given level of precision is a function of the variation within the population. Thus information from secondary sources may be used to ensure the desired level of precision. Furthermore, such information is necessary in order to determine the best allocation of a sampling budget.

Neyman (1934) provides a useful discussion of the use of prior information for allocating research budgets. The following simple illustration provides insight into the use of secondary sources for designing a sampling plan.

Consider the case of a population that is composed of several subgroups, each of which differs in variability along some dimension. One may wish to overrepresent the groups with greater variability while underrepresenting groups with lesser variation. Such a procedure is known as *stratified sampling*. For example, one might expect greater variations in the nature of discretionary spending in upper-income households than in lower-income households, as there is greater discretionary income available to the higher-income group. Thus oversampling of the high-income groups may be justified. Parameter estimates for the total population may be computed by correcting for the disproportionate sample sizes.

A related application of secondary sources is that of obtaining prior probability estimates for a particular event. Existing information may often be employed in conjunction with Bayes's theorem (a statistical theory) to reduce sample sizes required in further research. Because in many decision situations a high degree of precision is not required, a very small sample size (sometimes as few as 30) may be feasible if a priori estimates can be obtained. For example, an organization considering the introduction of a new service may be interested in the reactions of potential users of the service. By obtaining information on services with similar characteristics and benefits, it may be possible to obtain an estimate of the probability distribution of relative success of these services. Given this a priori distribution (previously obtained information), a small sample of potential users may be used to compute a revised probability of success that combines the prior information with the new information. A more complete discussion of the use of this methodology may be found in Wasson (1969).

Similarly, suppose that a company doing demographic research was interested in determining the standard deviation of the height of the female population for a particular neighborhood in Los Angeles. Let's assume that information on the height of females was *only* available in distributional form for the census tract encompassing the neighborhood. Using this existing information, one could obtain a quick "guesstimate" of the standard deviation for the neighborhood by (a) assuming a normal distribution of height and (b) using the height range for the census tract for which 10% of the population is shorter and 10% of the population is taller (i.e., between the tenth and ninetieth percentiles of height, which by definition represents 80% of the population). Let us assume that these heights are 51 inches and 59 inches, respectively. Using our first assumption of normality, then the difference in these numbers represents a spread of approximately 2.56 standard deviations (i.e., the approximate standard normal value for a symmetrical area on either side of the normal curve representing 80% of area is 1.28). Hence a quick guesstimate of the standard deviation for the height of the female population of this Los Angeles neighborhood is 59 inches minus 51 inches (i.e., 8 inches) divided by 2.56, which equals 3.125 inches.

Another use of existing information is the estimation of base rates. It is often useful to know something about the frequency of events or the probability that a particular characteristic will appear in a sample size of size n. Base rate information is particularly useful in designing studies of very specific populations. For example, knowing that the incidence of a medical disorder (e.g., cancer caused by chloroform in carbonated soft drinks) is only 1 in 1,000,000 suggests that such cases may be very difficult and expensive to identify with a sample random-sampling plan. Such base rate information is also important for ensuring that diagnostic and screening procedures do not detect large numbers of false positives (Overall & Klett, 1972).

Finally, prior research is useful for identifying testable hypotheses and new avenues of research. Research funds are spent most efficiently when new knowledge is gained as a result. An examination of secondary sources provides insight into what is and is not known, the limitations of previous research, the shortcomings of methodologies employed, and the generalizability of earlier conclusions. A thorough understanding of secondary source material is the basis for developing new primary research.

INTEGRATING SECONDARY SOURCE DATA

There is a long history of attempts to integrate existing information. Literature reviews, which exist in every academic discipline and are compiled routinely by organizations, represent such efforts at integration. The potential subjectivity of such integrative efforts was mentioned above. In addition, these efforts may also be biased by a failure to incorporate all of the information available or by an imprecise weighting of the conclusions from various sources (Cooper & Rosenthal, 1980). During the last 15 years, a number of authors have suggested that statistical procedures be used to integrate existing literature (Cohen, 1977; Cooper, 1979; Farley & Lehmann, 1986; Glass, 1976, 1977; Hedges & Olkin, 1985; Rosenthal, 1978, 1979; Rust, Lehmann, & Farley, 1990; Sheppard, Hartwick, & Warshaw, 1988; Tellis, 1988). These procedures have been referred to as *meta-analyses* (Glass, 1976, 1977; Hunter & Schmidt, 1989). Two volumes in this series discuss in detail how such integrative analyses are conducted (Cooper, 1989; Rosenthal, 1991). Recent applications of meta-analysis range from an examination of the price elasticity of selective demand to estimating publication bias to an examination of the effectiveness of the Fishbein and Ajzen (1975) model of attitude.

There are three basic approaches to integrating the findings of various sources. These approaches are by no means mutually exclusive; rather, they complement one another. The first and most obvious approach is to calculate simple summary statistics across a series of studies. The second approach involves integrating conclusions involving experimental and treatment effects obtained in independent studies. The third approach seeks to use differences in the way information was obtained, sampling differences, differences in how measures were operationalized, and so on to determine whether such differences had a significant impact on results obtained. These three approaches are described in greater detail in the following paragraphs.

The first approach, computing simple descriptive statistics, is useful for summarizing the findings of multiple studies. Means, variances, measures of association such as Pearson product-moment correlations, and other descriptive statistics may be combined. One method for accomplishing this type of integration is a simple weighted average. For example, assume four studies from various sources report the following mean daily television viewing by persons in the United States.

	Study 1	Study 2	Study 3	Study 4
Mean $\overline{X}$	5.3 hours	6.2 hours	4.8 hours	6.9 hours
Sample Size (n)	200	400	100	300

A simple average of the four means would yield a result of 5.8. But this figure would be somewhat misleading, because each mean is based on a different number of observations. Thus, to integrate the results, one should weight each individual mean by the number of observations upon which it is based, as follows:

$$\frac{(5.3)\,(200) + (6.2)\,(400) + (4.8)\,(100) + (6.9)\,(300)}{200 + 400 + 100 + 300} = \frac{6090}{1000} = \frac{6.09}{\text{hours}}$$

It is very important that one weight the results of studies by the number of observations to avoid being misled. In the above example, the results were not radically different, but consider a more extreme example:

	Study 1	Study 2
Mean $\overline{X}$	10	25
Sample size (n)	5	300

A simple average would yield an integrated mean of 17.5. The weighted mean would be 24.75. The weighting procedure is a simple device for placing greater emphasis on studies employing larger numbers of observations. Such weighting should also be carried out for proportions and measures of variability and association. Obviously, this weighting procedure does not account for differences other than in the number of observations. Other things being equal, however, weighting should be carried out routinely when integrating the results of multiple studies.

An even better approach to integrating descriptive statistics from multiple sources is the use of confidence intervals. Rather than arriving at a single summary statistic, the average of averages and information about means, sample size, and variability may be incorporated within a confidence interval. For example, instead of simply stating the weighted average of several results, a statement to the effect that the true mean lies between two values with a 95% probability may be made. For instance, the percentage of children with learning disabilities in a particular school district might be determined by studying a random sample of schoolchildren. Each child in the sample might be tested and the percentage of these children with learning disabilities used as an estimate of the incidence of learning disabilities in the total population of children. Suppose that a study was carried out, and the proportion of children with learning disabilities was found to be 15%. How much confidence might one place in this figure as an estimate of the percentage of children with these disabilities in the entire school district? One way to gauge confidence in the estimate is to compute a confidence interval. This would take the following form: The probability is .95 that the actual percentage of children with learning disabilities in the entire school district is between 13% and 17%.

The use of confidence intervals provides the user with a better "feel" for the data and helps to develop an appreciation for the fact that most numbers, no matter how sophisticated the procedures used to generate them, are only best guesses. The size of the confidence interval is influenced by many factors, including the size of the sample, the variability of the population, and the degree of confidence required by the researcher. Quite simply, as the space shuttle needs a wider and longer runway to ensure a successful landing with greater confidence, the researcher who requires greater confidence in his or her findings can accomplish this objective through a wider interval. Most elementary statistics texts include a discussion of confidence intervals.

The second basic approach to integrating the findings of various sources, which is to integrate the results of experimental studies, is more complex. Rather than simply developing summary statistics describing characteristics of multiple samples, the issue is one of how much support exists for the effect of a particular treatment condition on some outcome. Suppose that a school district is interested in the influence of a prekindergarten readiness program for disadvantaged children. Over the years, it may have conducted a number of studies that examined the effects of this program. In order to integrate the results of these studies, two questions must be raised. First, is there support for the hypothesis that the program affects future performance in the classroom? Second, if such influence is present, how strong is it? The first question is concerned with how to combine probability values associated with statistical tests. The second question involves estimating the variability accounted for by the effects.

When independent studies report tests of statistical significance, the probability values are important sources of information; they suggest the probability that some event could have occurred by chance alone. Statistical theory indicates that the probability of obtaining two independent events with probabilities P and Q is equal to the product PQ. Thus, if each of two studies rejects a null hypothesis at the .05 level (i.e., finds that real differences exist between two or more groups), the probability of obtaining two such events is $(.05)(.05) = .0025$, a rather rare event.

Consider the example of the prekindergarten readiness program above. Suppose that five studies have been carried out. Three found statistical support for the effect of the program (two studies at the .05 level, one at the .10 level) and two did not (both obtained probability values of .30), although the results were in the right direction. The probability of obtaining this combination of results by chance would equal $(.10)(.05)(.05)$ $(.30)(.30) = .0000225$, a very rare event. In many situations this simple product is not particularly helpful, because some studies may find support, others no support, and still others contradictory results. In such cases, more complex procedures are useful.

Edgington (1972a) has suggested a method for adding probabilities when the number of studies is small and the sum of the probabilities is less than 1. Winer (1971) and Mosteller and Bush (1954) have also suggested more sophisticated statistical methods for combining the results for several studies. These procedures have much to recommend them, but they become cumbersome with very large numbers of studies. In such cases, a simple counting method may be useful, although this method lacks the power of other methods. With this counting method, the number of studies finding a significant experimental effect is compared with the number that would be expected by chance alone.

A number of other procedures are also available for combining the results of independent studies. These have been reviewed and compared in papers by Rosenthal (1978) and Birnbaum (1954), and more recently in this series by Cooper (1989) and Rosenthal (1991). No one procedure appears to be best in all circumstances. Furthermore, even when such procedures suggest that particular effects may be attributable to some treatment condition(s), it is often of interest to determine the strength of the effect. Statistical significance alone does not suggest the practical importance of an effect.

There are two ways to present information on the size of an effect. One provides an estimate in terms of a correlation coefficient (the amount of variance associated with the effect); the other describes the effect in terms of a standard deviation unit (the size of the difference between outcomes when the treatment is applied versus when it is not applied). Integrating results of studies with regard to size of effect requires that information on effect size be present in each study. When this information is available, weighted averages of measures of association or difference measures provide a means for describing the strength of effects. Further discussion of such procedures may be found in Cohen (1969), Cooper (1989), Glass (1976, 1977), Glass, McGaw, and Smith (1981), Hunter and Schmidt (1989), and Rosenthal (1991).

The third and final approach to integrating research findings involves interpreting differences in the ways various studies were conducted. Differences among studies are a major source of confusion and variance when attempting to integrate findings. Variability in measures used, sampling frames, treatment effects, and even time of data collection serve to confound the interpretation of findings and the integration of results. It is possible, and even desirable, to examine the effects of both differences and agreements across studies.

One procedure for such analyses has been suggested by Snedecor and Cochran (1967; see also Cochran & Cox, 1957; Rosenthal, 1978). This procedure establishes each study (or study characteristic) as a treatment condition within an analysis of variance design. Means, sample sizes, and mean squares within treatment condition are then compared. Use of this procedure requires substantial information about the original research and a relatively large number of studies. This approach measures the treatment × studies interaction effect. Significant treatment × studies interactions suggest that the source of data makes a difference in the conclusions drawn. Further examination of such interactions may suggest that one class of studies (e.g., those that are well designed, or those using a particular subject population) tend to produce certain results, whereas other studies do not.

An interesting example of this type of analysis may be found in Farley et al. (1981) and has been extended since then by Sheppard et al. (1988). These researchers looked at studies of the Fishbein Behavioral Intention Model of attitude formation (Fishbein & Ajzen, 1975) in an effort to determine whether variations in research method, type of sample, discipline in conducting the research, and several additional parameters affected the findings reported by several studies. The results of the analyses reported in the first study provided rather strong support for the model under investigation and suggested that sampling and research method differences did not seem to have much impact on results. For example, it did not appear that the results of tests using students as research subjects differed markedly from results using other samples. It was also found, however, that results obtained by social psychologists provided stronger support for the model than research by investigators in marketing. This finding was particularly interesting given the differences in stimuli used and in method of presentation by researchers in these two disciplines, and it suggested several new research hypotheses. Sheppard et al. (1988) also found strong evidence for the predictive utility of the model. Most important, this research provided evidence to show that the model performed extremely well in the prediction of goals and in the prediction of activities involving an explicit choice among alternatives (two activities for which the model originally was not intended).

The analyses described above are called *generalizing from imperfect replication* and are very useful for integrating and synthesizing information. In addition, such analyses often suggest new research hypotheses and gaps in the existing literatures. For example, Sheppard et al. (1988) suggest that appropriate modification of the Fishbein and Ajzen (1975) model should begin "to account for goal intentions, choice situations, and differences between intention and estimation measures"

(p. 340). Glass et al. (1981) discuss other procedures for completing such metaanalyses and provide further illustrations of the technique.

SUMMARY

Information is useful only when it is applied to a particular problem or context and integrated into a meaningful pattern. The ability to synthesize is therefore an important skill. To do so requires the availability of information about the methodologies employed in the original studies and an understanding of the tools that aid such integration. Perfect information is seldom available. Thus the evaluation of information and the integration of findings across multiple sources become critical functions, functions that require research expertise as well as knowledge of information sources.

EXERCISES

Exercise 9.1: Five studies of the relationship between scores on a college admissions test and 4-year grade point averages (GPAs) produced the following results:

	Study 1	*Study 2*	*Study 3*	*Study 4*	*Study 5*
Correlation between test score and GPA	.42	.38	.91	.46	.39
Sample size	450	100	10	1500	1100

What would you conclude about the relationship between test scores and GPAs? What summary statistics would you employ to describe the results of these five studies? How do you explain the difference between the results of Study 3 and the other studies?

Exercise 9.2: Identify some areas of research where meta-analysis would be appropriate. What conditions must be met in order to perform a meta-analysis?

Exercise 9.3: For one of the areas identified in Exercise 9.2, attempt to complete a meta-analysis. What problems do you encounter? What conclusions can you draw?

References

Aaker, D. A., & Day, G. S. (1990). *Marketing research*. New York: John Wiley.

Abstracts in Anthropology. (quarterly). Farmingdale, NY: Baywood [1970].

Abstracts of Health Care Management Studies. (quarterly). Ann Arbor: Cooperative Information Center for Hospital Management Studies, School of Public Health, University of Michigan.

Abstracts of Hospital Management Studies. (annual). Ann Arbor: Health Administration Press for the Cooperative Information Center for Health Care Management Studies of the University of Michigan.

A citizen's guide on using the Freedom of Information Act and the Privacy Act of 1974 to request government records. (1989). Washington, DC: Government Printing Office.

Agricultural Prices. (monthly). Washington, DC: Department of Agriculture, Crop Reporting Board [1942].

Agricultural Statistics. (annual). Washington, DC: Department of Agriculture [1936].

Agriculture Outlook. (annual). Washington, DC: Department of Agriculture, Economic Research Service [1975].

Akey, D., Gruber, K., & Leon, L. (Eds.). (1983). *Encyclopedia of associations* (17th ed.). Detroit: Gale Research.

America: History and Life. Part A: Article Abstracts and Citation. (triannual). Santa Barbara, CA: American Bibliographical Center-Clio Press.

America: History and Life. Part B: Index to Book Reviews. (biannual). Santa Barbara, CA: American Bibliographical Center-Clio Press.

American Statistics Index: A Comprehensive Guide and Index to the Statistical Publications of the U.S. Government (annual; monthly and quarterly updates). Washington, DC: Congressional Information Service [1973].

Annual Register of Grant Support. (annual). Chicago: Marquis Who's Who.

Annual Survey of Manufacturers. (annual). Washington, DC: Bureau of the Census.

Anthropological Literature: An Index to Periodical Articles and Essays. (quarterly). Pleasantville, NY: Redgrave [1979].

Applied Science and Technology Index. (monthly). New York: H. W. Wilson.

Applied Science and Technology Index. (monthly, quarterly, annual cumulation). Edited by Joyce Howard. New York: H. W. Wilson.

Area Wage Survey. (annual). Washington, DC: Department of Labor, Office of Wages and Industrial Relations.

A Researcher's Guide to Washington. (annual). Washington, DC: Washington Researchers [1973].

AUBER Bibliography. (annual). Morgantown: Bureau of Business Research, College of Business and Economics, West Virginia University for the Association for University Business and Economics Research.

Barron's Market Laboratory. (annual). Edited by M. L. Farrell. Princeton, NJ: Dow Jones Books.

Bauer, D. (1970, June). The dimensions of consumer markets abroad. *Conference Board Record*.

Bibliographical Guide to Business and Economics. (annual). Edited by G. K. Hall. New York: New York Public Library, Research Library.

BI-DATA: Printout summary. (1980). New York: Business International.

Birnbaum, A. (1954). Combining independent tests of significance. *Journal of the American Statistical Association, 49,* 559-574.

BLS Handbook of Methods. (annual). Washington, DC: Bureau of Labor Statistics.

BLS machine readable data and tabulating routines. (1981). Washington, DC: Bureau of Labor Statistics.

Books in Print. (annual). New York: R. R. Bowker [1900].

Bourgue, P. J. (1974). Forecasting with input-output. In R. Ferber (Ed.), *Handbook of marketing research*. New York: McGraw-Hill.

Bradford's Directory of Marketing Research Agencies. (annual). Fairfax, VA: Bradford.

Bradford's Directory of Marketing Research Agencies and Management Consultants in the United States and the World. (annual). Fairfax, VA: Bradford.

British Overseas Trade Board. (1979). *International directory of published market research* (3rd ed.). London: Arlington Management Publications.

Business Conditions Digest. (monthly). Washington, DC: Bureau of Economic Analysis [1961].

Business ethics and responsibility: An information sourcebook. (1988). Written by P. A. Bick and edited by P. Wasserman. Phoenix, AZ: Oryx.

Business Index. (monthly). Menlo Park, CA: Information Access Corporation [1979].

Business information: A guide for librarians, students and researchers. (1988). By D. W. Strauss. Englewood, CO: Libraries Unlimited.

Business information: How to find it, how to use it. (1987). By Michael Lavin. Phoenix, AZ: Oryx.

Business information sources. (1985). Berkeley, CA: University of California Press.

Business International. (weekly). New York: Business International Corporation.

Business Periodicals Index. (monthly). New York: H. W. Wilson [1959].

Business reference sources. (1987). By L. M. Daniels. Cambridge, MA: Baker Library, Graduate School of Business, Harvard.

Business Statistics. (biennial). Washington, DC: Department of Commerce.

Catalog of Federal Domestic Assistance. (annual). Washington, DC: Office of Management and Budget.

Catalog of machine-readable records in the National Archives of the United States. (1977). Washington, DC: National Archives and Records Service.

Catalog of United States census publications, 1790-1945. (1968). Westport, CT: Greenwood.

Catalog of U.S. Census Publications. (quarterly). Washington, DC: Bureau of the Census.

Census and You. (annual). Washington, DC: Bureau of the Census.

Census catalog and guide. (1990). Washington, DC: Government Printing Office.

Census of agriculture. (1989). Washington, DC: Bureau of the Census.

Census of business. (1987). Washington, DC: Bureau of the Census.

Census of construction industries. (1987). Washington, DC: Bureau of the Census.

Census of governments. (1987). Washington, DC: Bureau of the Census.

Census of housing. (1990). Washington, DC: Bureau of the Census.

Census of manufacturers. (1987). Washington, DC: Bureau of the Census.

Census of mineral industries. (1987). Washington, DC: Bureau of the Census.

Census of population. (1990). Washington, DC: Bureau of the Census.

Census of retail trade. (1987). Washington, DC: Bureau of the Census.

Census of selected service industries. (1987). Washington, DC: Bureau of the Census.

Census of transportation. (1987). Washington, DC: Bureau of the Census.

Census of wholesale trade. (1987). Washington, DC: Bureau of the Census.

CIA world fact book. (1992). Washington, DC: Central Intelligence Agency.

Cochran, W. G., & Cox, G. M. (1957). *Experimental designs* (2nd ed.). New York: John Wiley.

Cohen, J. (1969). *Statistical power analysis for the behavioral sciences.* New York: Academic Press.

Cohen, J. (1977). *Statistical power analysis for the behavioral sciences* (rev. ed.). New York: Academic Press.

Colgate, C., Jr., & Fowler, R. L. (Eds.). (1983). *National trade and professional associations of the United States* (18th ed.). Washington, DC: Columbia.

Commerce Business Daily. (daily). Chicago: Administrative Services Office, Department of Commerce.

Communication Abstracts. (quarterly). Beverly Hills, CA: Sage.

Companies and Their Brands. (annual). Edited by D. Wood. Detroit: Gale Research.

Companies and Their Brands. (monthly). Washington, DC: Bureau of Industrial Economics.

Compendium of Social Statistics. (irregular). New York: United Nations [1963].

Consultants and Consulting Organizations Directory. (biennial). Detroit: Gale Research.

Consumers Index. (annual). Edited by C. E. Wall. Ann Arbor, MI: Pierian.

Cooper, H. M. (1979). Statistically combining independent studies: A meta-analysis of set differences in conformity research. *Journal of Personality and Social Research, 37,* 131-146.

Cooper, H. M. (1984). *The integrative research review: A systematic approach.* Beverly Hills, CA: Sage.

Cooper, H. M. (1989). *Integrating research: A guide for literature reviews.* Newbury Park, CA: Sage.

Cooper, H. M., & Rosenthal, R. (1980). Statistical procedures for summarizing research findings. *Psychological Bulletin, 87,* 442-449.

Corporate and Industry Research Reports Index. (annual, with quarterly supplements). Eastchester, NY: JA Micropublishing.

Corporate Profiles for Executives and Investors. (annual). Chicago: Rand McNally.

Corporation Records. (quarterly). New York: Standard & Poor's.

County and City Data Book: A Statistical Abstract Supplement (regions, divisions, states, countries, metropolitan areas, cities). (biannual). Washington, DC: Bureau of the Census.

County Business Patterns. (annual). Washington, DC: Bureau of the Census [1943].

Country Market Survey (CMS). (annual). Washington, DC: Department of Commerce, International Trade Administration.

Crop Production. (annual). Washington, DC: Department of Agriculture.

Crop Values. (annual). Washington, DC: Department of Agriculture.

Cultural directory: Guide to federal funds and services for cultural activities. (1975). New York: Associated Council for the Arts.

Current Construction Reports. (monthly). Washington, DC: Bureau of Industrial Economics.

Current Housing Reports. (annual). Washington, DC: Bureau of the Census.

Current Index to Journals in Education. (annual). Washington, DC: National Institute of Education.

Current Industrial Reports. (monthly). Washington, DC: Bureau of the Census.

Current Population Reports. (annual). Washington, DC: Bureau of the Census.

Database Directory. (1991). (annual). Edited by D. E. Woodworth & C. Goodair. White Plains, NY: Knowledge Industry.

Data Developments. (monthly). Washington, DC: Bureau of the Census.

Datapro directory of online services. (1983). Delron, NJ: Datapro Research.

Datapro directory of online services. (1991). Edited by B. Schepp. Delron, NJ: Datapro Research.

Defense Indicators. (monthly). Washington, DC: Bureau of Economic Analysis [1969].

Demographic Yearbook. (annual). New York: United Nations [1948].

Descriptive Supplement to Economic Indicators. (monthly). Washington, DC: Council of Economic Advisers.

Detailed input-output structure of the U.S. economy: 1977 volumes I and II. (1984). Washington, DC: Government Printing Office.

Digest of Educational Statistics. (annual). Washington, DC: National Center for Education Statistics [1962].

Direct marketing in Japan. (1990). Edited by K. Takahashi. Tokyo: Dodwell Marketing Consultants.

Directories in print. (1991). Edited by C. B. Montner. Detroit: Gale Research.

Directory Information Service Guide. (triannual). Detroit: Information Enterprises.

Directory of American Firms Operating in Foreign Countries. (annual). New York: World Trade Academic Press.

Directory of data files. (1989). Washington, DC: Bureau of the Census.

Directory of data sources on racial and ethnic minorities. (1975). Washington, DC: Bureau of Labor Statistics.

Directory of directories. (1983). Detroit: Gale Research.

Directory of European associations. (1976). Detroit: Gale Research.

Directory of federal statistical data files. (1981). Washington, DC: National Technical Information Service and Office of Federal Statistical Policy and Standards.

Directory of industry data sources: The United States of America and Canada. (1981). Cambridge, MA: Ballinger.

Directory of International Statistics. (1982). New York: United Nations.

Directory of occupational titles. (1962; 1975 update). Washington, DC: Department of Labor.

Directory of on-line databases. (1991). Detroit: Gale Research.

Directory of On-Line Data Bases. (1991). (quarterly). Edited by J. C. Barg. Los Angeles: Cuadra.

Directory of On-Line Information Resources. (biennial). Kensington, MD: CSG [1978].

Directory of On-Line Information Resources. (semiannual). Detroit: Gale Research.

Directory of on-line portable databases. (1991). Detroit: Gale Research.

Directory of United Nations information systems and services. (1991). New York: United Nations.

Disability statistics compendium. New York: United Nations.

DiscAmerica. Warwick, NY: Compact Publications.

Dissertation Abstracts International: Abstracts of Dissertations Available on Microfilm or as Xerographic Reproductions. (annual/monthly). Ann Arbor, MI: University Microfilms International [1938].

Doing business in Canada. (1979). New York: Price Waterhouse.

Dow Jones averages 1885-1970. (1972). Princeton, NJ: Dow Jones Books.

Dow Jones Investor's Handbook. (annual). Homewood, IL: Dow Jones-Irwin.

Dun & Bradstreet Million Dollar Directory. (annual). New York: Dun & Bradstreet.

Dun & Bradstreet Principal International Businesses. (annual). New York: Dun & Bradstreet.

Dun's business rankings. (1982). New York: Dun & Bradstreet.

Dun's Financial Profiles. (custom). New York: Dun and Bradstreet.

Dun's Guide to Israel (annual). Edited by D. Dephina. Tel Aviv: Dun & Bradstreet.

Dun's service companies. (1991). Parsippany, NJ: Dun's Marketing Services.

Economic Indicators. (monthly). Washington, DC: Council of Economic Advisers.

Economic Indicators of the Farm Sector. (annual). Department of Agriculture, Economic Research Service [1979].

Economic Report of the President. (annual). Washington, DC: Office of the President of the United States.

Edgington, E. S. (1972a). An additive method for combining probability values from independent experiments. *Journal of Psychology, 80,* 351-363.

Edgington, E. S. (1972b). A normal curve method for combining probability values from independent experiments. *Journal of Psychology, 82,* 85-89.

Education Index. (monthly). Edited by M. C. Hewitt. New York: H. W. Wilson.

EIA Data Index: An Abstract Journal. (biannual). Washington, DC: Energy Information Administration [1980].

EIA Establishments. (custom). New York: Economic Information Systems.

EIA Plants. (custom). New York: Economic Information Systems.

EIA Publications Directory: A User's Guide. (semiannual). Washington, DC: Energy Information Administration [1980].

Employment and Earnings. (monthly). Washington, DC: Bureau of Labor Statistics.

Employment and Earnings Statistics for States and Areas. (annual). Washington, DC: Bureau of Labor Statistics [1939].

Employment and Earnings Statistics for the United States. (annual). Washington, DC: Bureau of Labor Statistics [1909].

Encyclopedia of Associations. (biennial). Detroit: Gale Research. [1982].

Encyclopedia of business information sources. (1988). Edited by J. Wov. Detroit: Gale Research.

Encyclopedia of geographic information sources. (1986, U.S. volume; 1988, international volume). Edited by J. Mossman. Detroit: Gale Research.

Encyclopedia of Geographic Information Sources. (annual). Edited by J. Mossman. Detroit: Gale Research.

Engineering Index. (monthly). New York: Engineering Index.

Eskin, G. (1981, September 18). Advances in scanner based research systems yield fast, accurate new product test results. *Marketing News,* p. 20.

Ethnic statistics: A compendium of references sources. (1978). Arlington, VA: Data Use and Access Laboratories.

Ethnic statistics: A compendium of references sources. Washington, DC: Department of Commerce, National Technical Information Service.

Ethnic statistics: Using national data resources for ethnic studies. (1978). Arlington, VA: Data Use and Access Laboratories.

Europe's 15,000 Largest Companies. (annual). Edited by A. Humphries. London: ELC International, Ealing.

F & S Index, Europe. (annual, quarterly, monthly). Cleveland: Predicasts [1978].

F & S Index International. (annual, quarterly, monthly). Cleveland: Predicasts [1980].

F & S Index to Corporations and Industries. (annual, quarterly, monthly, weekly). Cleveland: Predicasts [1960].

Farley, J. U., & Lehmann, D. R. (1986). *Meta-analysis in marketing: Generalizing from response models.* Lexington, MA: Lexington Books.

Farley, J. U., Lehmann, D. R., & Ryan, M. J. (1981). Generalizing from imperfect replication. *Journal of Business, 54,* 597-610.

Farley, J. U., Lehmann, D. R., & Ryan, M. J. (1982). Patterns in parameters of buyer behavior models: Generalizing from sparse replication. *Marketing Science, 1,* 181-204.

Federal Budget in Brief. (annual). Washington, DC: Office of Management and Budget [1951].

Federal Evaluations. (irregular, last published 1980). Washington, DC: General Accounting Office.

Federal Register. (daily). Washington, DC: Office of the Federal Register.

Federal Register Index. (monthly). Washington, DC: Government Printing Office.

Federal Reserve Bulletin. (monthly). Washington, DC: Board of Governors of the Federal Reserve System [1915].

Federal Reserve Chart Book. (quarterly). Washington, DC: Board of Governors of the Federal Reserve System [1947].

Federal Reserve Historical Chart Book. (annual). Washington, DC: Board of Governors of the Federal Reserve System [1947].

Federal Statistical Directory. (annual). Washington, DC: Office of Management and Budget [1951].

FINDEX: The Directory of Market Research Reports, Studies and Surveys. (annual). Edited by J. Duchez & S. J. Marcus. Bethesda, MD: Cambridge Information Group.

Fishbein, M., & Ajzen, I. (1975). *Belief, attitude, intention and behavior: An introduction to theory and research.* Reading, MA: Addison-Wesley.

Fiske, D. W. (1971). *Measuring the concepts of personality.* Chicago: Aldine.

Forbes Report on American Industry Issue. (annual). Edited by J. W. Michaels. New York: Forbes.

Foreign Agricultural Trade of the United States. (monthly). Washington, DC: Department of Agriculture, Economics, Statistics, and Cooperatives Service [1962].

Foreign Agriculture. (monthly). Department of Agriculture, Foreign Agricultural Service [1963].

Fortune Directory. (annual). Edited by E. Benjamin. New York: Time.

Fortune Double 500 Directory, Fortune Magazine (May-August, annual). New York: Time.

Fowler, F. J., Jr. (1988). *Survey research methods.* Newbury Park, CA: Sage.

Freedom of Information Act: What it is and how to use it. Washington, DC: Freedom of Information Clearinghouse.

Glass, G. V. (1976). *Primary, secondary, and meta-analysis of research.* Paper presented at the meeting of the American Educational Research Association, San Francisco.

Glass, G. V. (1977). Integrating findings: The meta-analysis of research. *Review of Research in Education, 5,* 351-379.

Glass, G. V., McGaw, B., & Smith, M. L. (1981). *Meta-analysis in social research.* Beverly Hills, CA: Sage.

Guide to American directories (10th ed.). (1978). Coral Springs, FL: B. Klein.

Guide to American scientific and technical directories (2nd ed.). (1975). Coral Springs, FL: B. Klein.

Guide to Foreign Trade Statistics. (annual). Washington, DC: Government Printing Office.

Guide to Grant and Award Programs. (annual). Bethesda, MD: National Institutes of Health.

Guide to USDA statistics. (1973). Washington, DC: Department of Agriculture.

Haas, R. W. (1977). SIC systems and related data for more effective market research. *Industrial Marketing Management, 6,* 429-435.

Handbook of Basic Economic Statistics. (annual; monthly supplements). Washington, DC: Economic Statistics Bureau.

Handbook of cyclical indicators. (1977). Washington, DC: Department of Commerce, Bureau of Economic Analysis.

Handbook of Labor Statistics (annual). Washington, DC: Bureau of Labor Statistics [1926].

Handbook of Latin American Studies. (annual). Austin: The University of Texas Press [1935].

Health Industries Handbook Annual. (annual). Palo Alto, CA: SRI International.

Hedges, L. V., & Olkin, I. (1985). *Statistical methods for meta analysis.* Orlando, FL: Academic Press.

Hedrick, T., Bickman, L., & Rog, D. (1992). *Planning applied research.* Newbury Park, CA: Sage.

Henry, G. (1991). *Practical sampling.* Newbury Park, CA: Sage.

Highlights of U.S. Export and Import Trade. (Monthly). Washington, DC: Department of Commerce [1967].

Hispanic American Periodicals Index. (annual). Los Angeles, CA: UCLA Latin American Center Publications [1975].

Historical Abstracts. (quarterly). Santa Barbara, CA: American Biographical Center [1955].

Historical Chart Book. (annual). Federal Reserve System, Board of Governors [1965].

Historical statistics of the United States: Colonial times to 1970. (1975). Washington, DC: Bureau of the Census.

Honomichl, M. (1990, May 28). The Honomichl 50: The 1990 Honomichl business report on the marketing research industry. *Marketing News,* pp. H1-H30.

Housing and Urban Development Statistical Yearbook. (annual). Washington, DC: Department of Housing and Urban Development [1969].

Humanities Index. (quarterly). New York: H. W. Wilson. [1974].

Human Resources Abstracts: An International Information Service. (quarterly). Newbury Park, CA: Sage [1966].

Hunter, J. E., & Schmidt, F. L. (1989). *Methods of meta-analysis: Correcting error and bias in research findings.* Newbury Park, CA: Sage.

Index Medicus. (monthly). Bethesda, MD: National Library of Medicine.

Index to Health Information. Bethesda, MD: Congressional Informational Service.

Index to International Public Opinion. (1988-1989). (annual). Westport, CT: Survey Research Consulting International and Greenwood Press.

Index to Latin American Periodical Literature. (annual). Boston: G. K. Hall [1929-1969].

Index to legal periodicals. (1979). Washington, DC: George Washington University.

Index to 1990 census summary tapes. (1992). Washington, DC: Bureau of the Census.

Index to selected 1990 census reports. (1992). Washington, DC: Bureau of the Census.

Indexes to International Statistics: A Guide to the Statistical Publications of International Intergovernmental Organizations. (annual). Bethesda, MD: Congressional Informational Service [1983].

Industrial research laboratories of the United States (15th ed.). (1977). New York: Bowker.

Industrial Statistics Yearbook. (1991). New York: United Nations.

Information Industry Directory. (annual). Edited by B. J. Morgan. Detroit: Gale Research.

Insurance Periodicals Index. (annual). New York: Insurance Division, Special Libraries Association.

International Bibliography of Social and Cultural Anthropology. (annual). New York: Tavistock [1955].

International Business Year Book. (annual). London: Financial Times.

International Directory of Market Research Companies and Services. (annual). Edited by M. Allen. New York: American Marketing Association.

Irregular serials and annuals: An international directory (8th ed.). (1983). New York: Bowker.

Katzer, J., Cook, K. H., & Crouch, W. W. (1978). *Evaluating information: A guide for users of social science research.* Reading, MA: Addison-Wesley.

Kelley, J., & McGrath, J. (1988). *On time and method.* Newbury Park, CA: Sage.

Kelly's Business Directory. (annual). Windsor, CT: Reed Information Services.

Kelly's Manufacturers and Merchants Directory. (annual). Kingston upon Thames, UK: Kelly's Directories.

Local Area Personal Income. (annual). Washington, DC: Department of Commerce, Bureau of Economic Analysis.

Local area personal income 1971-76. (1978). Washington, DC: Bureau of Economic Analysis.

Long term economic growth: 1860-1970 (2nd ed.). (1973). Washington, DC: Bureau of Economic Analysis.

Lutz, G. M. (1983). *Understanding social statistics.* New York: Macmillan.

Maloney, J. F. (1976, July 2). In Saudi Arabia, sands, statistics can be shifty. *Marketing News,* p. 6.

Management Contents. (biweekly). Skokie, IL: G. D. Searle [1975].

Marketing Economics Key Plants: Guide to Industrial Purchasing Power. (annual). Edited by A. Wong. New York: Marketing Economics Institute.

Marketing information: A professional reference guide (2nd ed.). (1987). Atlanta: Georgia State University College of Business Administration.

Marketing Information Guide. (monthly). Garden City, NY: Hoke Communications.

Market Research Abstracts. (semiannual). London Market Research Society [1963].

Marketsearch: International Directory of Published Market Research. (annual). Edited by K. Mann. Arlington, VA: Arlington Management Publications

Master Key Index. (quarterly). New York: Business International Corporation.

May, E. G. (1979). *A handbook for business on the use of government statistics.* Charlottesville, VA: Taylor Murphy Institute.

Measuring markets: A guide to the use of federal and state statistical data. (1979). Washington, DC: Industry and Trade Administration, Department of Commerce, Bureau of the Census.

Mediamark Research. (annual). New York: Mediamark Research.

Mental Health Abstracts. (monthly). Rockville, MD: National Clearinghouse for Mental Health Information, National Institute of Mental Health [1969].

Merchandising. (annual). New York: Billboard.

Monthly Bulletin of Statistics. (monthly). New York: United Nations [1947].

Monthly Catalog of U.S. Government Publications. (monthly). Washington, DC: Government Printing Office [1895].

Monthly Labor Review. (monthly). Washington, DC: Bureau of Labor Statistics [1915].

Monthly Report on the Labor Force. (monthly). Washington, DC: Bureau of Labor Statistics.

Monthly Retail Trade. (monthly). Washington, DC: Bureau of the Census.

Monthly Selected Service Receipts. (monthly). Washington, DC: Bureau of the Census.

Monthly Vital Statistics Report. (monthly). Hyattsville, MD: Department of Health and Human Services, Public Health Service.

Monthly Wholesale Trade: Sales and Inventories. (monthly). Washington, DC: Bureau of the Census.

Moody's Manuals. (annual, with supplements). New York: Moody's Investors Service.

Mosteller F. M., & Bush, R. R. (1954). Selected quantitative techniques. In G. Lindzey (Ed.), *Handbook of social psychology: Vol. 1. Theory and method.* Cambridge, MA: Addison-Wesley.

National environmental statistical report. Washington, DC: National Technical Information Service.

National Technical Information Service. (1975). *National environmental statistical report.* Arlington, VA: Mitre Corp.

National Trade and Professional Associations of the United States and Canada and Labor Unions. (annual). Washington, DC: Columbia.

Natural Gas Monthly. (monthly). Washington, DC: Department of Energy, Office of Oil and Gas [1983].

New York Times Index. (semimonthly). New York: New York Times [1913].

Neyman, J. (1934). On the two different aspects of the representative method: The method of stratified sampling and the method of purposive selection. *Journal of the Royal Statistical Society, 97,* 558-606.

Nichols, P., & Van Den Elshout, R. (1990, February). Survey of databases available on CD-ROM: Types, availability, and content. *Database, 13,* 18-23.

NIH Research Contracting Process. (annual). Bethesda, MD: National Institutes of Health.

Norback, C. T. (1980). *Corporate publications in print.* New York: McGraw-Hill.

Occupational Outlook Handbook. (biennial). Washington, DC: Department of Labor, Bureau of Labor Statistics [1949].

Overall, J. E., & Klett, J. C. (1972). *Applied multivariate analysis.* New York: McGraw-Hill.

Pas, H. T. V. (1973). *Economic anthropology, 1940-1972: An annotated bibliography.* Osterhout, Netherlands: Anthropological Publications.

Personnel Management Abstracts. (quarterly). Ann Arbor: Graduate School of Business Administration, University of Michigan.

Petroleum Marketing Monthly. (monthly). Washington, DC: Department of Energy, Office of Oil and Gas [1983].

Petroleum Supply Annual. (annual). Washington, DC: Department of Energy, Office of Oil and Gas [1981].

Pick's Currency Yearbook. (annual). New York: Pick.

Population Bibliography. (bimonthly). Chapel Hill: University of North Carolina, Carolina Population Center [1966].

Predicasts Forecasts. (annual, quarterly). Cleveland: Predicasts.

Price Waterhouse Guide Series. (annual). New York: Price Waterhouse.

PRIZM adds zip to consumer research. (1980, November 10). *Advertising Age,* p. 22.

Progressive Grocer. (monthly). Stamford, CT: MacLean Hunter Media.

Projections of Educational Statistics. (annual). Washington DC: National Center for Education Statistics. [1962].

Psychological Abstracts: Nonevaluative Summaries of the World's Literature in Psychology and Related Disciplines. (monthly). Arlington, VA: American Psychological Association [1927].

Public Affairs Information Service Bulletin: A Selected Subject List of the Latest Books, Pamphlets, Government Publications, Reports of Public and Private Agencies and Periodical Articles, Relating to Economic and Social Conditions, Public Administration and International Relations, Published in English Throughout the World. (monthly). New York: Public Affairs Information Service. [1914].

Publication Yearbook. (annual). Rome: Food and Agriculture Organization of the United Nations.

Quarterly Operating Data of Telegraph Carriers. Washington, DC: Federal Communications Commission.

Quarterly Operating Data of Telephone Carriers. Washington, DC: Federal Communications Commission.

Raymondo, J. C. (1989, January). How to estimate population. *American Demographics, 11,* 34-35.

Reader's Guide to Periodical Literature. (semimonthly). New York: H. W. Wilson. [1900].

Reichmann, W. J. (1962). *Use and abuse of statistics.* New York: Oxford University Press.

Riche, M. F. (1991). The 1991 directory of marketing information companies. *American Demographics* (supplement).

Rosenthal, R. (1978). Combining results of independent studies. *Psychological Bulletin, 85,* 185-193.

Rosenthal, R. (1979). The "file drawer problem" and tolerance for null results. *Psychological Bulletin, 86,* 638-641.

Rosenthal, R. (1984). *Meta-analytic procedures for social research.* Beverly Hills, CA: Sage.

Rosenthal, R. (1991). *Meta-analytic procedures for social research* (rev. ed.). Newbury Park, CA: Sage.

Rosenthal, R., & Rubin, D. B. (1979). Comparing significance levels of independent studies. *Psychological Bulletin, 86,* 1165-1168.

Rust, R. T., Lehmann, D. R., & Farley, J. U. (1990, May). Estimating publication bias in meta analysis. *Journal of Marketing Research, 27,* 220-226.

Sage Public Administration Abstracts. (quarterly). Newbury Park, CA: Sage [1974].

Sales and Marketing Management. (monthly). New York: Sales and Marketing Management [1918].

Schwartz, J. (1989, January). Back to the source. *American Demographics, 2,* 22-26.

Science Citation Index. (quarterly). Philadelphia: Institute for Scientific Information [1969].

Science Indicators. (biennial). Washington, DC: National Science Board [1972].

Sheldon's Department Stores. (annual). Edited by K. W. Phelon, Jr. Fairview, NJ: Phelon, Sheldon & Marsar.

Sheldon's Retail Directory of the United States and Canada. (annual). New York: Phelon, Sheldon & Marsar.

Sheppard, B. H., Hartwick, J., & Warshaw, P. R. (1988, December). The theory of reasoned action: A meta analysis of past research with recommendations for modifications and future research. *Journal of Consumer Research, 15,* 325-343.

Singer, M. (1971). The vitality of mythical numbers. *Public Interest, 23,* 3-9.

Smith, M. L., & Damien, Y. M. (Eds.). (1982). *Anthropological bibliographies: A selected guide.* South Salem, NY: Redgrave.

Snedecor, G. W., & Cochran, W. G. (1967). *Statistical methods* (6th ed.). Ames: Iowa State University Press.

Social Science Index. (monthly). New York: H. W. Wilson [1974].

Social Sciences Citation Index: An International Multidisciplinary Index to the Literature of the Social, Behavioral, and Related Sciences. (quarterly). Philadelphia: Institute for Scientific Information [1973].

Sociological Abstracts. (monthly). San Diego: Sociological Abstracts [1952].

Source Book for Criminal Justice Statistics. (annual). Washington, DC: National Criminal Justice Information and Statistics Service [1973].

Standard & Poor's Register of Corporations, Directors, and Executives. (annual). New York: Standard & Poor's.

Standard & Poor's Stock Reports. (annual). New York: Standard & Poor's.

Standard industrial classification manual. (1990). Washington, DC: Office of Management and Budget.

Standardized micro-data tape transcripts. (1976). Washington, DC: National Center for Health Statistics.

Standard periodical directory. (1981). Edited by M. Manning. New York: Oxbridge Communications.

Standard Rate and Data Service. (monthly). Skokie, IL: Standard Rate and Data Service.

Statesman's Yearbook. (annual). London: Macmillan [1864].

Statistical Abstract of the United States. (annual). Washington, DC: Bureau of the Census.

Statistical Reference Index. (annual). Washington, DC: Congressional Information Service [1980].

Statistical services of the United States government (rev. ed). (1975). Washington, DC: Office of Management and Budget, Statistical Policy Division.

Statistics of Income. (annual). Washington, DC: Internal Revenue Service [1916].

Statistics of the Communications Industry in the U.S. (annual). Washington, DC: Federal Communications Commission [1939].

Statistics Sources. (1989). Edited by J. Wasserman O'Brien & S. R. O'Brien. Detroit: Gale Research.

Sudman, S., & Ferber, R. (1979). *Consumer panels.* Chicago: American Marketing Association.

Supplement to Economic Indicators. (monthly). Washington, DC: Council of Economic Advisers.

Survey of Current Business. (monthly). Washington, DC: Bureau of Economic Analysis [1921].

Tax, S., & Grollig, F. X. (1982). *Serial publications in anthropology 1982.* South Salem, NY: Redgrave.

Tellis, Gerard J. (1988, May). Advertising exposure, loyalty, and brand purchase: A two-stage model of choice. *Journal of Marketing Research, 25,* 134-144.

The input-output structure of the U.S. economy. (1984, May). *Survey of Current Business,* pp. 42-78.

Thomas Register of American Manufacturers. (1991). (annual). Edited by R. J. Duchane. New York: Thomas.

Trade and Industry Index. (monthly). Menlo Park, CA: Information Access [1981].

Trade Directories of the World. (monthly). Queens Village, NY: Croner.

Ulrich's International Periodicals Directory. (biennial). New York: Bowker.

Unemployment in States and Local Areas. (monthly). Washington, DC: Department of Commerce, Bureau of Economic Analysis [1976].

UNESCO Statistical Yearbook. (annual). Paris: United Nation Educational, Scientific, and Cultural Organization [1963].

Uniform Crime Reporting. (quarterly). Washington, DC: Federal Bureau of Investigation.

Uniform Crime Reports for the United States. (annual). Washington, DC: Federal Bureau of Investigation [1980].

United Nations Statistical Yearbook. (annual). New York: United Nations [1949].

United States Government Manual. (annual). Washington, DC: Office of the Federal Register, General Services Administration.

United States Political Science Documents. (annual). Pittsburgh: University of Pittsburgh [1975].

Urban Affairs Abstracts. (weekly; quarterly and annual cumulations). Washington, DC: National League of Cities [1971].

U.S. Bureau of the Census. (1990). *TIGER: The coast-to-coast digital map base.* Washington, DC: Author.

U.S. Crude Oil, Natural Gas, and Natural Gas Liquid Reserves. (annual). Washington, DC: Department of Energy, Office of Oil and Gas [1977].

U.S. Government Purchasing and Sales Directory. Washington, DC: Government Printing Office.

U.S. Industrial Outlook. (annual). Washington, DC: Industry and Trade Administration.

Value Line Investment Survey. (quarterly; weekly supplements). New York: A. Bernhard.

Van Willigen, J. (1982). *Anthropology in use: A bibliographic chronology of the development of applied anthropology.* South Salem, NY: Redgrave.

Vital Statistics of the United States. (annual). Washington, DC: National Center for Health Statistics [1937].

Vital Statistics Report. (monthly). Washington, DC: Department of Health and Human Services.

Wall Street Journal Index. (monthly). Princeton, NJ: Dow Jones Books [1957].

Wasserman, P., & Morgan, J. (Eds.). (1978). *Consumer sourcebook.* Detroit: Gale Research.

Wasserman, P., O'Brien, J., Grace, D. A., & Clansky, K. (Eds.). (1982). *Statistics sources* (7th ed.). Detroit: Gale Research.

Wasserman, P., Sanders, J., & Sanders, E. T. (1978). *Encyclopedia of geographic information sources* (3rd ed.). Detroit: Gale Research.

Wasson, C. (1969). *Understanding quantitative analysis.* New York: Appleton-Century-Crofts.

Wasson, C. (1974). Use and appraisal of existing information. In R. Ferber (Ed.), *Handbook of marketing research.* New York: McGraw-Hill.

Wasson, C. R., & Shreve, R. R. (1976). *Interpreting and using quantitative aids to business decision.* Austin, TX: Austin.

Weekly Petroleum Status Report. (weekly). Washington, DC: Department of Energy, Energy Information Administration [1981].

Weiss, M. J. (1988). *The clustering of America.* New York: Harper & Row.

Wheeler, M. (1977). *Lies, damn lies and statistics.* New York: Dell.

Who Owns Whom. (annual). Editorial Manager: Steve Birtles. Buckinghamshire, UK: Publications Division, Dun & Bradstreet.

Who's Who in America. (biennial). Chicago: Marquis Who's Who.

Williams, M. E. (1991). *Preface to Computer Readable Databases: A Directory and Sourcebook* [annual]. Edited by K. Y. Marcaccio. Detroit: Gale Research.

Winer, B. J. (1971). *Statistical principles in experimental design* (2nd ed.). New York: McGraw-Hill.

Work Related Abstracts. (monthly). Detroit: Information Coordinators.

World Advertising Expenditures. (annual). New York: Starch INRA Hooper.

World Agricultural Supply and Demand Estimates. (monthly; quarterly supplements). Washington, DC: Department of Agriculture [1973].

World Agriculture Situation and Outlook Report. (quarterly). Washington, DC: Department of Agriculture, Economic Research Service [1942].

Worldcasts. (quarterly). Cleveland: Predicasts.

World Economic Survey. (annual). New York: United Nations [1947].

World Health Statistics Annual. (annual). General: World Health Organization [1969].

World Statistics in Brief. (annual). New York: United Nations [1976].

Yearbook of Agriculture. (annual). Department of Agriculture [1980].

Author Index

Subject Index

About the Authors

David W. Stewart (Ph.D., Baylor University) holds the Robert E. Brooker Chair in Marketing at the University of Southern California. Prior to moving to Southern California, he was Senior Associate Dean and Associate Professor of Marketing at the Owen Graduate School of Management, Vanderbilt University. He is a past President of the Society for Consumer Psychology and a Fellow of both the American Psychological Association and the American Psychological Society. He has authored or coauthored more than 100 publications and six books: *Secondary Research: Sources and Methods, Effective Television Advertising: A Study of 1,000 Commercials, Consumer Behavior and the Practice of Marketing, Nonverbal Communication in Advertising, Focus Groups: Theory and Practice*, and *Advertising and Consumer Psychology*. His publications have appeared in the *Journal of Marketing Research, Journal of Marketing, Journal of Consumer Research, Management Science, Journal of Advertising, Journal of Advertising Research, Academy of Management Journal, Journal of Applied Psychology, Journal of Health Care Marketing, Journal of the Royal Statistical Society*, and *Current Issues and Research in Advertising*, among others. He serves on the editorial boards of 10 professional journals, including both the *Journal of Marketing* and the *Journal of Marketing Research*. His research has examined a wide range of issues, including consumer information search and decision making, advertising effectiveness, methodological approaches to the analysis of marketing data, and marketing strategy. His research and commentary are featured frequently in the business and popular press.

Michael A. Kamins (Ph.D., New York University) is Associate Professor of Marketing at the University of Southern California. He has authored more than 15 articles on marketing. His work has been published in the *Journal of Marketing Research, Journal of Marketing, Journal of Advertising Research*, and the *Journal of the Academy of Marketing Science*, among others. His research interests lie in explaining the cognitive and affective responses to advertising, as well as advertising puffery. The impact of his research efforts on the business world has been written about in the *Wall Street Journal* and the *Los Angeles Times,* among other publications.